SEA BEARS

The Story of the Fur Seal

FREDERICKA MARTIN

SEA BEARS

The Story of the Fur Seal

CHILTON COMPANY — BOOK DIVISION
Publishers
Philadelphia   New York

To Tobyanne, my Pribilof-born daughter

Preface

I met the Alaskan fur seals in 1941, a year of crisis in the history of the animals, and, before I left the island of St. Paul, in the Bering Sea, my country, too, faced a tragic crisis. The war came close to our island in that early summer of 1942. As the fur seals swarmed northward, they came home to islands being hastily prepared for military defense. But the sealers were not there to see them land. Nor was I. From the deck of the ship carrying the sealers and Government personnel southward out of the danger zone, I had my last glimpse of the Pribilof seals. The world was ablaze with violent battles, but, obedient and tractable to ancestral laws, the fur seals were hurrying northward—as usual.

Neither absence nor the flight of time has dulled my memories of the sea bears' favorite beaches, and the bonds of friendship forged between me and the Pribilof Islanders during my year's stay with them have not only been preserved but also strengthened by constant correspondence. Because fur sealers and the fur seals still retain their strong hold on my heart and mind, it is a great pleasure to retell their story.

The story of the ruthless hunting of the fur seals of the Southern Hemisphere has been retold here in a more condensed form than in my previous book, *The Hunting of the Silver Fleece,* in order to relate more fully the events which led to the protection and survival of their Alaskan cousins and to bring the story of the latter up to date.

Since Alaska has achieved statehood, curiosity about the people and the natural resources of the forty-ninth state deserves satisfaction. The Aleuts, who have obtained a livelihood from fur seals for generations, comprise but a small community compared to the Alaskan Indian peoples and Eskimos. But size of population is no measure of worth or interest. The Aleut sealers have their own niche in American history. Because of their dependence on the fur seal, to write of the animal is to write of the people whose survival has depended on it.

Minerals and timber may be more commercially important, but no profitable Alaskan resource is so picturesque and romantic as the Pribilof Island herd of Alaska fur seals, the strange animals whose skins are among the most elegant and stylish of furs today. The peculiar history of this animal should become as familiar to young Americans as the epic of the Plains buffalo, especially because the preservation of Alaska's sea bears will one day be one of their responsibilities as citizens.

FREDERICKA MARTIN

Acknowledgments

For assistance in helping me to assemble the latest information for this retelling of the sea bears' story, I owe most to Dr. A. Henry Banner, oceanographer on the staff of the University of Hawaii, whom I first met on St. Paul Island in 1941, and to Dr. Victor Scheffer and Mr. Ford Wilke, Fish and Wildlife Service scientists. I am very grateful to the Secretary-Treasurer of the American Society of Mammalogists, Mr. Brian P. Glass, for helping me locate the authors of many fur seal studies of the last decade, and to Prof. George A. Bartholomew of the University of California and Mr. E. H. McEwen, a Canadian wild life biologist, for sending me reprints of their fur seal studies.

For the original inspiration to write an account of fur sealing, published as *The Hunting of the Silver Fleece,* and much information about the Alaska fur seal, I am indebted to the Aleut American sealers I lived among on St. Paul Island, largest of the Pribilof Islands, in the Bering Sea, from June 1941 to June 1942, and to many Aleut Americans from Attu, Atka, and Unalaska. Correspondence with these friends has kept me informed, during the years since I last saw them, of the changing conditions of the sealers' way of life, and the Village Council of St. Paul Island gladly sent me a detailed account of their gains and the problems that still beset them, to use in this book. There are no words to express my feelings about bonds of friendship and helpfulness which have worn so well for so long a passage of time.

So many of those Pribilof friends and teachers as well as officials of the Fish and Wildlife Service and members of their families who were my fur seal mentors have died during the intervening years that remembering their kind, often affectionate, attentions is painful to me. I regret especially that Mr.

Ward T. Bower, former Chief of Alaska Fisheries, and that enthusiastic and tireless interpreter of fur seal matters, Mr. Edward C. Johnston, former Superintendent of the Pribilof Islands, who conducted me on my first unforgettable tour of a fur seal beach, will not see this book.

To two residents of St. Paul, The Reverend Makary Baranov and his wife, my debt is immense. Particularly interested in the Russian and ecclesiastical history of the Seal Islands, Father Baranov has recovered and preserved many old documents and has recorded whatever oral Pribilof tradition the local Aleuts remember. His files were invaluable, but his enthusiastic, stimulating companionship as a fellow researcher was even more precious and inestimable. I thank the former Pribilof radio operator, Mr. Elvin Elliott, and his genial wife, Inez, not only for many favors rendered me on St. Paul but also for permission to reproduce several of their seal photographs in this book.

Dr. Vilhjalmur Stefansson helped me in innumerable ways. Not the least of his kindnesses was his introduction to the great linguist and scholar, the late Mr. Richard Henry Geoghegan, who permitted me to use his unpublished translations of Russian books containing the earliest written history of the Aleuts and the northern fur seals. His death denied me the privilege of showing him the use I made of his studies, and this public acknowledgment of his assistance seems so trifling a tribute to his memory that it affords me little comfort. The contributions of Dr. John P. Harrington, the former Senior Ethnologist of the Smithsonian Institution, have been many, varied, and very important.

For courtesy, patience, and helpful suggestions, I wish to thank many librarians—they must, unhappily, be anonymous—on the staffs of the National Archives, the Library of Congress, the New York Public Library, and the American Museum of Natural History. I thank the latter Museum for the privilege of reproducing the photograph of the elephant seal. The photographs of St. Paul sealing activities were furnished by the Department of the Interior.

FREDERICKA MARTIN

Introduction

If the history of the fur seal were presented in novel form, it would be dismissed as fantasy. It would be too dramatic; it would contain too many climaxes and anticlimaxes telescoped one on the other, and would leave the reader unbelieving. But the saga of the furry beasts that brought wealth, fame, turmoil, and tragedy to those who knew them, though stripped of all embroidery, still retains the components of a lusty melodrama.

Fredericka Martin combines her first-hand knowledge of the Pribilof Islands and its inhabitants with a thirst for research, and gives us a bold and honest account of the fur seal. She has woven the varicolored threads of exploration, history, biology, politics, and ethnology into a stout, rich fabric. Her sympathetic picture of the present-day Aleuts is a story that badly needed telling. She has told it well.

EVELYN STEFANSSON
Lecturer in Northern Studies, Dartmouth College

Contents

SEA BEARS

The Story of the Fur Seal

1

The Long Masquerade

Foredestined by its fur to ultimate commercial eminence, the fur seal was defrauded of a formal and dignified introduction to history by early European intruders into its territory, who mistakenly regarded it as a seal. Their blunder deprived the fur seal of a proper name for centuries, and, because of it, the animal still bears a clumsy, inappropriate appellation. The fur seal is not a seal. Morphologically, this sea animal is more closely related to the land bear than to the hair seal. But visitors stopping off at fur seal beaches on their way to the New World, to the Indies, to Cathay and Cipango, were too fevered with visions of more dazzling and conspicuous wealth to distinguish separate animal species among the tumultuous crowds of sea lions, fur seals, and varieties of true seals swarming along the same strip of seacoast. The fur seal's unique personality, its facile land motion, each physical characteristic which marked its generic difference from other aquatic mammals, the Europeans ignored.

The fur seals appeared deceptively ordinary and worthless; their ash-gray, earth-brown pelts blending dully with the harsh, fire-riven rocks of their beach havens, their short velvet underfur partially obscured by longer, stiff, unsightly guard hairs. Misled by their slight resemblance to true seals, even mariners who disturbed fur seals on land and killed them for food, accepted them as commonplace, familiar acquaintances. Avid fortune hunters tramped carelessly across thronged fur seal beaches

1

to fill their casks inland with fresh water, impatiently thrusting the living furs from their paths, ironically unaware of the wealth that brushed against their boots.

Although nearly every successive voyage into strange waters of the Southern Hemisphere after the discovery of the Cape of Good Hope in 1488 inadvertently charted a course to more fur seal retreats, this mistaken identity continued to disguise the fur seals. To the newcomers there was nothing spectacular or unusual about a mere seal, nothing new to learn about so well-known a creature. The early Greeks had known seals and had named a city Phocaea in their honor. Aristotle had described the seal's anatomy and physiology completely and for all time and had classified it as an intermediate member of the animal family, a creature belonging to no one element, at home on land and in the sea.

Generations of northern Europeans had made their livelihood killing seals, principally for their fat. The Anglo-Saxon bards had sung of the sea as the "Seal Bath" and the "Seal's Path." Before missionaries brought old Greek and Roman learning to the North, the primal inhabitants of the region had called seals "nickers" or "nicors," the same name the walrus and evil sea spirits bore. Sixteenth- and seventeenth-century eyes gazed smugly at the hair seal, the elephant seal, the sea lion, and the fur seal in the Southern Hemisphere and, their vision straitened by the limited knowledge of their era, saw but a single animal, the seal.

First of the marine mammals to impress the purblind Europeans and win a separate, identifying title was the sea lion. Its leonine head and shoulders quite naturally inspired the name. But trespassers, who had been violently expelled from a sea lion rookery, recalled the gleam of the animals' prominent pointed bicuspids, and called them sea wolves. The recognition of the sea lion roused no curiosity about its neighbors. The less conspicuous, more amiable and placid fur seal continued to be obscure and unmolested.

This much the misnomer afforded the fur seals. It delayed

for generations their persecution by man the fur hunter. The ancestors of the fur seals had assured their descendants a tranquil existence by settling only the loneliest, least populated regions of the world. Whether this isolation was deliberate choice or accident is impossible to determine. In a more recent period the fur seal revealed itself too habit-bound, too enslaved by custom, to save itself by flight from its land residence and the ruthless killers who lay in wait along its rookery borders. Yet when the fur seals established their breeding communities, their instinct of self-preservation may have been keen and active, not blunted by generations of disuse. Certainly that hoary evolutionary scandal perpetrated by the fur seals' progenitors might have been the outcome of a self-defensive caution that bordered on cowardice.

The fur seals' lineage can be traced far back into a biologic era in which their forebears were wholly terrestrial and probably closely related to the ancestors of the land bears of today. At a fateful date obscured by the passage of millenniums, this land animal began to descend from its high biologic status and creep back for security to the elemental abode of life, the sea. Perhaps a natural catastrophe—either a prolonged drought or the advance of glacial ice relentlessly overrunning its habitat— left that primordial precursor nowhere to flee save the sea. Possibly larger, more aggressive animals harried it until existence on land was untenable. Or excessive timidity may have impelled it to retreat instead of advance, to shrink from danger instead of confronting and overcoming it; and, having pulled the animal most of the way back to aquatic life, the same fear may have dictated its choice of isolated breeding beaches.

No matter the stimuli which prompted the regression, the evolutionary retreat is established fact. The body of the living fur seal today exhibits stunted organs, such as finger bones and nails, and vestigial pelvic and sinus structure and other features which demonstrate its ancestors' adaptation to existence on land. The most significant confirmation of its biological history is the fact that at birth the baby fur seal is still a land animal,

unfit for aquatic existence. Only after persistent and arduous
practice can a young fur seal conquer sea currents and be at
home in the ocean. But when its sea apprenticeship is over, the
fur seal is become a creature of dual habitat, spending two
thirds of its life among the waves and one third ashore. Had
fatal events not altered the fur seal's destiny, it might today be
a furred beast of the land. Instead, it is a creature poised mid-
way between two animal worlds, chained to earth by the duties
of nourishing terrestrial offspring, its sea life only a recess from
obedience to nature's inexorable command to be fruitful and
multiply.

Where those ancient land ancestors of the fur seal lived is
unknown. The few fossil fragments of related ancestral species,
discovered to date only in Miocene deposits in the Pacific area,
have merely invoked controversial speculation as to whether
the fur seal evolved in the North Pacific or the Pacific sub-
antarctic. No trustworthy fossil evidence indicates that either
the evolving fur seal or its progenitors ever inhabited the North
Atlantic. It seems a certitude that the first fur seals to settle in
the South Atlantic emigrated, some few thousand years ago,
from Pacific beaches. Wherever the first fur seals achieved their
individuality as members of the Otariidae or eared seal family,
a branch of the finned-footed Pinnepedia clan, one fact seems
clear. In time the originally small ancestral group or groups became a prolific flourishing dynasty which had outgrown its
birthplace. Gradually groups departed in search of better
stocked fishing grounds and less crowded beaches for mating
and bringing up their land-bound young. Again and again small
bands split off from the main stock or, as breeding space became cramped, from the more recently settled colonies, and
wandered until they found new, congenial resorts. In time, after
long residence apart, herds acquired peculiar characteristics
and underwent physical modifications which divided the original
family order into distinct species.

The failure of the fur seal or its progenitors to settle the
North Atlantic kept Europeans from meeting its descendants

until Diaz showed the way south to the Cape of Good Hope
and Columbus opened up the New World, and other navigators,
penetrating unknown seas to the south, came at last into the
great water domain of the Pacific. Hardly a vessel left a European port bound for unpredictable destinations, seeking more
knowledge of the world, that did not cross the sea lanes of
the fur seals or skirt their land stations. For the magnitude of
the fur seal's territory was impressively vast when Europeans
began their explorations.

Consider the boundaries and extent of the realm of the southern genus, the bear-headed fur seal, commencing near the
northern border of Uruguay on the Coronilla Islands, a little
to the south on the Castillos Grandes and the Lobos Islands
in the broad estuary of the Rio de la Plata. Withdrawn from the
settlements of the "Big Feet," as Magellan nicknamed the tall-
statured aborigines, their rookeries were scattered along the
Patagonian coast to the very tip of South America. On many
islands of the archipelago of Tierra del Fuego, particularly on
Staten Land, fur seals resided, their populations scarcely disturbed by the raids of their primitive human Fuegian neighbors. Still farther south, within the zone of Antarctic storms,
the seals with the thickest, most opulent fur of their genus occupied rookeries on the New Shetland Islands, and smaller herds
shared beach space with elephant seals on Elephant Island and
the South Orkneys.

Northward along the western coast of South America the fur
seal had colonized secluded mainland beaches and the islands
of St. Mary and the Chiloe groups. Westward in the Pacific,
opposite Valparaiso, fur seal millions congregated on famous
Juan Fernandez and Más Afuera and less abundantly on St.
Felix and St. Ambrose farther north. Fur seals inhabited many
isles of the Galapagos Archipelago, north and south of the
Equator; and above that median line, the Guadaloupe Islands,
tiny isolated Clipperton and the Farallones Rocks opposite San
Francisco Bay—even, it has been claimed, the California headland of Cape Mendocino and Oregon's Cape Blanco.

The clusters of islands south and southwest of New Zealand contained large fur seal communities: Chatham and Bounty, the Antipodes and the Aucklands, Campbell and Macquarie, and many others. Fur seal rookeries bordered Bass Strait between Tasmania and Australia; and in the south Indian Ocean they were numerous on the coasts of New Amsterdam and St. Paul. In the Indian Ocean, too, on shores washed by the Antarctic current, seals possessing exceptionally thick and beautiful furs carried on their procreative duties on Prince Edward and Marion Islands, the Crozet Group and chill, forlorn Kerguelen Land. A few small rookeries of fur seals were crowded between the hosts of elephant seals on Heard Island.

At the extremity of the African continent, on the western mainland as well as on scattered coastal islands, fur seals possessed rookeries.

The most northerly Atlantic outpost of the fur seals may have been Ascension Island. St. Helena, Napoleon's prison at a later date, was once a fur seal haven as, in mid-Atlantic, were the islands of Tristan da Cunha and Gough. Bouvet, the Sandwich Islands, South Georgia, and the Falklands were also their purlieus.

This southern or Antarctic genus, which ringed the southern half of the globe with its breeding haunts, was divided into more species than can be determined today. But the Viking species, the fur seals of the North Pacific, remained a single great three-branched clan: one branch occupied the bleak Kuril Islands and Robben Island north of Japan; another had taken possession of the two large Commander Islands; while the third laid claim to the lava-bouldered shores of the Pribilof Islands in the Bering Sea.

Widely outflung across the world, the fur seals' thousand resting places were as infinitely varied as the globe itself—as bleak as sullen Kerguelen, first called Desolation Land; as tropical as Juan Fernandez with its cabbage palms, and the equatorial, sun-scorched Galapagos rocks; as barren as the South Shetlands, where only thin grasses pushed up between the harsh rocks; as wooded with evergreens as some isles of Tierra del Fuego; as gloomily caverned as Nightingale of the da Cunha group; as fog-curtained and wind-hammered as St. Paul in the Bering Sea. To each seal island its fur seal residents came, sojourned, and returned happily to the sea when their land duties were completed. They were among the more carefree animal denizens of the universe. Beset by only one dangerous animal enemy, the killer whale, victimized by few diseases and parasites, their principal foes were the storms which buffeted too roughly the very young and very old animals. This halcyon existence was not disturbed by the first harbingers of civilization whose dim vision pronounced them mere seals. But not forever could the seal guise conceal their silver-shaded, silky, fleece-like fur . . .

2

"A Creature Pretty Well Known"

The fur seal was certainly mentioned in the sixteenth- and seventeenth-century logs of Spanish, Portuguese, Dutch, and other European mariners, as well as in narratives of the English explorers and buccaneers. Since neither the writers nor their contemporary readers were aware of its presence in their texts or in the universe, the detection of their references to the fur seal is extremely difficult. Only occasionally are there geographical allusions or other hints to aid the searcher. Undoubtedly fur seals were among the "certaine sea-wolves, commonly called with us Seales," which Drake, Cavendish, Withrington, Lister, John Davis, and other English sea-rovers killed for fresh meat on the islands at the mouth of the River Plate and farther down the South American coast at Port Desire. But this is the judgment of hindsight. English seamen from Elizabeth's reign to that of George II remained unaware that they dined on animals destined to high, though tragic, commercial fame. Perhaps Sir Francis Drake and his nephew who, according to the Spanish prisoner confined on the *Golden Hind,* the pilot Da Silva, painted all new "birds, trees, and sea lions" encountered in their travels, may have painted the fur seal's portrait, but no trace of Drake's report and illustrations has ever been found.

The earliest unmistakable reference to fur seals was penned by a homesick Hollander in command of a Dutch fleet attempting the conquest of Chile and Peru. Off Staten Land in March 1646, Captain Hendrik Brouwer listened to the bleating cries of brown sea lions and gray sea dogs—cries that sounded "not unlike our sheep." Had his heart not yearned for a homeland he was never to see again—he conquered only enough Chilean earth for his own grave—he might have paid no attention to brown male and gray female fur seals, the only adult marine animals to bleat like sheep. Almost 200 years later the grandfather of the poet Byron found the striking difference in color and size between adult male and female fur seals most confusing. Commodore Byron had heard of fur seals, but he mistook the adult male for the mother and the bevy of smaller, gray females for her offspring, and spread the fallacious report that fur seals had numerous offspring—as many as eighteen infants to one litter. The commodore's error was serious, for a mother seal produces only one infant each season.

Because mariners of all nations depended on the flesh of aquatic animals for food and oil, the latter required for their "butter" and for greasing shipgear, many references to "Seales" occur in the records of the first 150 years of European exploration. And it was Europe's need for more "trane-oyle," the liquid fat of sea mammals, which instigated the first forays against "Seales" in the Southern Hemisphere.

Just when Europeans began to depend on the animal residents of the South Atlantic for oil is not known. Instructions given an oiling expedition in 1583 indicate it was no pioneer undertaking. The *Edward Cotton* was to pick up salt for preserving hides at the Cape Verde Islands, proceed to Santos and St. Vincent to lay in fresh victuals and to trade, and finally to the Plate "to make their voyage by the traine, and hides of the seales with such other commodities as are there to be had . . ." Master Cotton gave "Marchant" Cheeseman written orders to trade for amber, sugar, green ginger, and other Brazilian com-

modities but "touching the making of the traine [blubber oil]
and preserving of the hides I leave it wholly to the order and
discretion of the chiefe of the Companie."

The rambling title of the narrative as Hakluyt, the English
historian, preserved it ends: ". . . which perished through ex-
treme negligence neare Rio Grande in Guinie, 17 of July,
1583." Because a tale of shipwreck always commands an audience, only the stark tragedies of such dull mean trade, like the
Edward Cotton disaster, were recorded. Had Cheeseman succeeded in getting seal hides and oil—assuredly fur seal oil and
skins would have been part of the cargo, Hakluyt would have
ignored his venture. Histories of profitable oiling voyages were
too commercially vulgar to please a public surfeited with tales
of grandiose sea exploits, of fabulously rich treasure hauls.

Where Master Cotton expected to dispose of his seal hides,
Hakluyt's narrative, of course, does not state. Did English tan-
ners clip off the fur seal pelt's guard hairs as the Chinese did
later and cure the thick hide along with hair seal and sea lion
skins? Considering the fondness of the Elizabethan court for
furs, it would be ironical if the dehaired, tanned pelts of the fur
seal were being made up into homely leatherwares such as
luggage, purses, or belts, into apprentices' leather aprons, into
the rough jerkins and doublets of the common people.

In contrast to the practical, hardheaded English who, unin-
terested in their differences, were quick to find a commercial
use for all "Seales," the Spaniards, although no better natural
scientists, were inclined to regard sea beasts with superstitious
awe. The weird, fierce battle between men and animals which
occurred in 1618 on one of the seal islands in Port Desire, was
a conflict so apocryphal that its human participants could only
have been men who believed in griffons, unicorns, and dragons.

An expedition commanded by the two De Nodal brothers
anchored at Port Desire for fresh water. On an islet in the bay
a landing party surprised some sleeping sea lions. Their own
account cannot be surpassed:

"Jumping on land, we saw a male and a female, and ap-

proached them with two lances and an arquebus; Captain Nodal
had a small ax in his hand. The male was asleep and the female
watching. As we came near, she gave loud noises enough to
cause fear. Feeling the lances, the male turned toward the
female, biting her, and because he had awakened or because
he understood that the lances would injure them, they both
plunged from a rock into the sea. We attacked another male
with lances . . . An artilleryman, a Fleming, had the arquebus
and Captain Nodal held the small ax, about three feet long.
When the sea lion was wounded with the lances, it rose on its
feet higher than a man, uttering loud cries. Its size, strength,
and ferocity were fearful. It seized a lance head in its teeth
and using the iron as a dart gave Captain Gonzalo de Nodal
such a cut across the cheek that he could not eat nor heal his
wound for more than a month. He was striking it on the head
with his ax and twice the sea lion tore the ax from his hands
with his teeth. It was impossible to kill it, until the Fleming
loaded the arquebus with two balls and shot it in the head. It
then fell and we renewed our attack until at last we killed it,
being all tired from the combat."

Not willing to be bested by the lions of the sea, the Spaniards
secured reinforcements.

"After we arrived a second time with the boats, the multitude
of these animals was so great, their ferocity, size, form, and
color so strange, and the noise they made so deafening owing
to their numbers, that it gave rise to fear and horror. We
jumped on shore with our weapons and began a skirmish with
them. If it had not been for the arquebuses, it would not have
been possible to land. It was wonderful to see their resolution
in defense of their females and the young, the males always
placing themselves in front, where there was the greatest danger. They had the females in such subjection that if they showed
a desire to go into the sea, they bit them and forced them to
stay on shore. It was indeed astonishing to see how these animals defended their females and young ones. We also saw the
females take the young in their mouths and carry them to the

males, never parting from their males, so that they formed one body with the males, fighting fiercely when they wanted to get near them. Except with the arquebuses we could not do them any harm."

It is remarkable that the superstitious Spaniards did not flee in horror from animals so mysteriously protected, save their heads, from the arqubuses' lead balls. That the density of the animals' thick blubber stopped the shot they could not have realized. Before dusk they had killed a hundred adult sea lions and many nervous youngsters who had bolted from their mothers straight toward the raiders' lances. Because each body, as large as a bullock, required a half dozen men to roll it over, only five skins were carried from the field as souvenirs of the mighty contest. The Spaniards took a few young animals aboard but, annoyed by their incessant, goatish bleating, they soon tossed them overboard.

Flashes in the tale—a reference to black skins, to the female's resemblance to white sheep—seem to indicate that the narrator, despite the melee, caught sight of fur seals. Unless accidentally embroiled in the fighting, they must have been spectators, maintaining, since it was mating season, their beach stations and adding only their voices to the tumult.

Suddenly, toward the close of the 17th century the fur seal found two biographers. The enormous herd of fur seals on Juan Fernandez Island in the Pacific Ocean attracted, for different reasons, the attention of a mariner named Simson or Simpson and the famous English buccaneer and explorer, William Dampier. Both began to strip the animal of its seal disguise.

Simpson kept the journal of the voyage of the English vessel, the *Welfare,* which anchored off Juan Fernandez in 1689 to take aboard water and fresh food. Running his hand along a fur seal's back, Simpson sank his fingers deep into its soft underfleece. The clinging, silky hairs whispered to him of great fortune. If this skin could only be felt, he was confident it would answer "all ye ends of beaver furr." His captain agreed. But the pelts they stowed aboard the *Welfare,* doubtless scorned by London furriers, immediately disappeared from history. Simpson's prophetic narration was banished to the manuscript vault of the British Museum, unpublished. The beaver's position in the fur mart remained unchallenged.

Dampier singled out the fur seal for practical reasons and published its first description in his *Voyages Around the World* very hesitantly. Because "the Seals are a Sort of Creature pretty well known," he apologized, "yet it may not be amiss to describe them." As he delineated a creature so different from the familiar seal of popular and scientific knowledge, nascent doubts intruded into his factual reporting. Mark his words: "They are as big as Calves, the head of them like a Dog, therefore called by the Dutch the Sea Hounds . . . Their Hair is of divers Colours as black, grey, dun and spotted looking, very sleek and pleasant when they come first out of the Sea; for these at John Fernando's have fine, thick, short fur; the like I have not taken notice anywhere but in these Seas." Hair was adequate to describe seals but, for the particular seals of Juan Fernandez, only the word "fur" was appropriate. And across his mind sped the shadowy suspicion that they were not exactly like the well-known creatures. "Here are many Seals; they come up to sun themselves only on two or three of the Islands. I don't know whether exactly of the same kind with those in Colder Climates, but . . . they always live where there is Plenty of Fish." Fish! Had he not been so interested in noting the latitudes where seals, and invariably plenty of fish, congregated, Dampier might not have mentioned the lowly, familiar seal in his journal.

It was not insult enough that the unfortunate fur seal was forced to masquerade so long as the common seal. Making its debut in print, it was dragged in apologetically only as a guide to good fishing. Writing over a decade before Linnaeus and Buffon were born, Dampier at least described the fur seal so accurately that naturalists examining his words in their European studies were certain that his seal was either a new species of seal or a wholly different aquatic creature.

In 1694 a Dr. Grew found, in the collection of the Royal
Society's Museum in London, a dusty, dried, neglected fur seal
skin, an anonymous gift dated 1686. So mystifying was his
attempted reconstruction of the animal it had once clothed that,
more than a hundred years later, Baron Cuvier, trying to fit the
re-created animal into his own system of natural history, ex-
claimed in despair, "What shall I make of this seal?"

Dampier's assumption that sealing was too well-known an
occupation to merit inclusion in his narrative is, at this date,
most exasperating. He was familiar with seal oiling, even with
the trade value of seal pelts. He noted that large ships could
load quickly with skins and oil at Juan Fernandez because the
seals were "extraordinary fat." If he thought the Fernandez
seals' thick blubber warranted long, hazardous voyages to Juan
Fernandez Island, evidently, long before the close of the 17th
century, oiling was a steady and extremely profitable occupation
for the English. His reference only increases the mystery that
surrounds the beginnings of European sealskin commerce and
inspires unanswerable speculations about the possible employment of fur seal leather in England.

The Spaniards, by Dampier's day, were killing all kinds of
seals for oil, often crudely melting the blubber by dropping hot
stones among fatty tissues laid in an earth pit, as the Indians
did. Like mariners and buccaneers, they used the purest oil for
"butter"; the less refined for tanning. The skins may have been
tanned for sandals and other useful articles, but certainly their
furlike quality was never suspected.

For almost a century after Dampier, before a profitable market for seal furs was discovered, the English quietly continued
and increased their seal oil operations. A few vessels from other
countries—Germany and Holland, probably also from French
and Scandinavian ports—tried seal oiling. Every beast or fowl
possessed of a shred of fat went into the try pot. Thousands of
fur seals must have been boiled down on many a lonely beach
in the Southern Hemisphere. If seal oilers as optimistic as
Simpson bore pelts home to sell, they found no buyers as furs.

So clumsy were the first faltering accounts of the fur seal that, despite the increasing intimacy between oilers and fur seals, its formal scientific introduction was delayed for another half century after Dampier's book was published; its commercial recognition still longer.

3

Steller Discovers the Sea Bears

Homeward bound for Siberia from his second and final exploration of the North Pacific, Vitus Bering's ship, the *Saint Peter,* was wrecked in November 1741, on the coast of a remote island in a lonely sea; both named Bering in his honor. To one survivor, the official naturalist of the expedition, the wreck afforded an opportunity to become a great scientist-discoverer. George William Steller's mission to collect American flora and fauna had been frustrated by Commander Bering's refusal to anchor off unknown coasts. Then autumn storms intervened and the winds drove the *Saint Peter*—and Steller—to the shores of an uninhabited island teeming with unknown or scarcely known animals. Sick and forlorn, sustained only by the hope that they had landed on the Kamchatkan mainland, the castaways put up makeshift shelter and reconnoitered for food, plagued day and night by impudent blue foxes. They grew more despondent as one by one the scurvy victims, including their great captain, died.

Organizing his fellow Germans into a personal entourage, Steller helped them build the sturdiest huts and taught them to make palatable, healthful meals with whatever was available. His conviction that they were on an unknown island did not

16

Two Curious Pups Look on While a Cow Rebuffs the Photographer

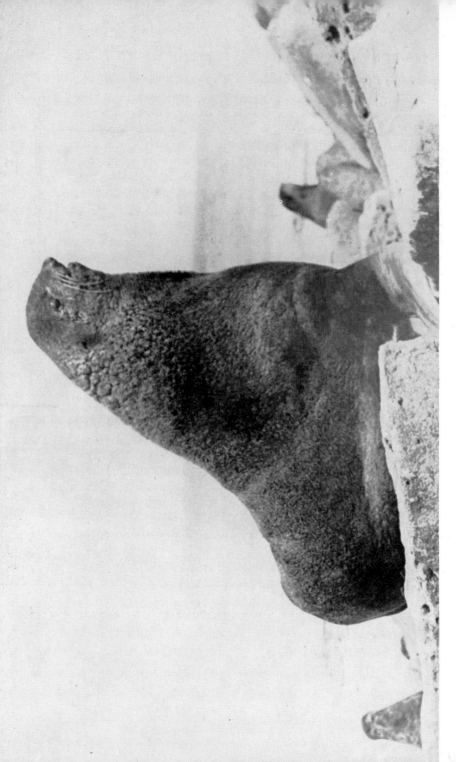

A St. Paul Beachmaster Waiting for His Summer Mates

trouble his scientific spirit as he settled down to study the animal residents of his asylum.

Throughout the winter sea otters lingered offshore. The sea cow, that derelict sea beast, lay, moored helplessly by its enormous bulk, in coastal waters. Doomed to be exterminated before 1763 by Russian visitors to the Commander Islands, Steller's description and drawings are the sole account of this strange animal. In the spring a host of sea lions—a few young males had patrolled the coast all winter—came ashore to breed.

In the spring, too, came the "sea cats," as the first Russians in Kamchatka had nicknamed the fur-coated seallike animals which twice a year passed the Siberian coast without landing. At last the fur seal encountered a human being capable of recognizing its generic character, a scholar who knew how to draw up dignified Latin credentials to proclaim its identity. The nickname "sea cat" Steller rejected as misleading; "sea bear" was biologically a more accurate name.

Before the first sea bear arrived, the little band of Russians had been losing heart. Exploring parties reported water north, south, east, and west of their camp. Marooned on an island with their food almost gone, an unmeasured sea separated them from Kamchatka. The very size of the captured sea bear cheered them; its flesh, they judged, would feed the whole company for a week. Undismayed by the rank steam curling up from their plates, they sat down gratefully to dine on fur seal on Easter Sunday, April 18, 1742, according to the old Russian calendar. Their celebration of the holy festival was marred by its aftermath. The fetid odor, which Steller called the "smelle of hellebore," offended their stomachs. "There were hardly any of the men who did not have to vomit and lost all their appetite." The sea, however, soon provided succor. The following Tuesday, the carcass of a whale, newly dead and consequently edible, was cast ashore; it stocked their larder for some weeks.

As the specter of starvation reappeared, the female fur seals arrived, and their flesh proved palatable. Better still was the tender meat of their newborn infants—as tasty, thought Steller, if properly prepared, as roast suckling pig; fur seal tongues and hearts even more delicious.

During May and June the survivors built from the remains of the *Saint Peter* a small boat to bear them homeward. With few useful tools and no skilled workers—the ship's carpenters had died of scurvy—they were sustained in their labors by their fur seal diet.

Steller was busier than the shipbuilders. The fur seals came only to the southern shore, a long, tiresome overland journey from their camp. ". . . this is a curious fact, that the sea bears are not found everywhere on the shores of their islands, as are the sea cows, the seals, the otter and the sea lions, but only on the southern shore which faces Kamchatka. The reason for this is obvious—for they see this part of the island first when they come on their journey eastward from Camp Kronotski." Back and forth Steller tramped, collecting plants along the way, watching for new birds and insects, and toting home for the community a load of seal meat.

When Steller's detailed description of the sea bears was published, few familiar European animals had an equally comprehensive biography. In his field notes, so well written that little polishing was required before publication, he mentioned the fur seal's first biographer, the English buccaneer who had partially lifted its seal mask. "Dampier has given us a description of this animal, called *Kot* by the Russians, which is, to be sure, brief and imperfect; but he mentions its characteristics so definitely and plainly and so clearly at first sight that I cannot doubt that the animal is his 'sea bear.' "

Steller's conclusions were cautious. ". . . Dampier says of the Island Ferdinand . . . that there upon the land he found the whole shore covered with countless herds of seals, sea bears, in the same way as we found it in Bering Island. This does not lead me to believe that these animals come hither from those southern latitudes, for this distance would be far too great, but I gather from it two facts: first, that the sea beasts of the Southern Hemisphere are the same, or not very different, from those of the Northern in about the same longitude; and second, it is credible that our sea bears spend the winter in about the same degree of north latitudes."

Methodically he commenced the study of his sea bears, killing and dissecting a six-year-old male on May 28, a momentous date in the development of natural history. On that lonely seacoast one of the most brilliant scientists of his day bent over the steaming carcass of an animal known only to the inattentive seamen of southern latitudes, to Kamchatkan tribes, and another few thousand scattered aborigines, and bared its anatomical secrets. In his wind-blown laboratory, Steller plied his knife with such painstaking exactness that he obtained the dimensions even of the sea bear's smallest internal organs. In turn he dissected the bodies of female and young animals. Erecting a small hut on an elevation in the rookery's heart to observe the great drama of the living seals, day after day and for one continuous period of six days, night and day, he looked down on the frenzied swirl of animal life that surrounded his observation tower and recorded in vivid phrases the sea bear's eccentric behavior. Errors in his account are, judged even by the scientific standards of our times, negligible and due mainly to his short stay on Bering Island. His most serious defect was his attribution of sensitive emotions to an animal particularly devoid of parental and romantic sensibilities because, in common with the naturalists of his century and long afterward, he endowed all animals with human reasoning powers and emotional reactions. So his sea otters displayed vanity over their personal appearance, his sea lions umpired the sea bears' boxing matches, his voiceless sea cows seemed to sigh as if they were wounded, and his sea bears were loving parents.

As lover, husband, and father, the male seal which Steller portrays is chivalrous, tender, and protective; the female an adoring wife and devoted mother. Unfortunately for baby fur seals, such parents exist only in the pages of his narrative. Few mammalian parents are so indifferent to their young, so cold and mechanical in the performance of their breeding duties.

"Although many thousands of them lie upon the shore together, yet it may always be observed that they are separated into families—the one male lies with his wives, his sons, and daughters, as also his yearling sons who are not yet old enough to have a harem. One family often numbers as many as 120 . . . The males are polygamous; one often has eight, fifteen, or even fifty wives. He guards them with anxious jealousy . . . ," Steller wrote. Only the season's newborn, the offspring of other fathers, and his temporary summer wives— a seraglio of over a hundred furred odalisques is not unknown as he stated—surround each beachmaster. There is scant likelihood that a cow will be captured by the same bull for two successive seasons. Just as rare, then, is the birth of a pup in his own father's harem. The family group is a season's gathering; its members bound by no ties of concern or affection.

The pregnant female which the Russians called *matka,* mother, coming in from her winter feeding to give birth to her pup, meets no tender welcome. Small, about one fifth the size of a bull, the pretty silver-furred creature, her soft coat stained with creamy, rufous patches, must, in obedience to an instinctive warning of imminent birth pains, run the gantlet of ravening males that line the water front. Frequently dragged from the surf, tossed roughly back and forth by excited males, escaping the harsh bites of one bull only to be snatched up in the jaws of another, eventually she is forcibly settled as a member of her captor's harem.

In the vortex of animal motion, jostled by restless or stampeding cows and sporting pups, carelessly knocked about by her fighting spouse, for a day or two the harassed female waits the advent of her young. If she seeks to flee, she is either bitten and mauled and tossed back on her master's rocks, or borne off by a raiding neighbor. Passively, she endures the pangs of labor in the same mad, noisy atmosphere. Little wonder she neither licks nor caresses her newborn infant.

Unlike most animal mothers she is not a midwife. The pup, a small elastic ball of fat, garbed in a shining black, thin-haired pelt, staggers at once to his unsteady flippers. For several days —until the edges of the rocks have worn away the withering umbilical cord—he drags after him the placenta that may still be nourishing him. The cow does, of course, nurse her pup, but she submits stolidly, coldly, and is unfriendly, even pettily mean in rebuffing his inquisitive nuzzling. Beyond suckling her nursling, a fur seal mother takes no responsibility for her offspring's upbringing and exhibits no concern for his safety.

His stepfather is neither guardian nor protector. Crossly the bull cuffs or snaps at luckless pups who get in his way, heedlessly tramping or sitting on them. Fortunately harem duties keep a bull so busy he rarely settles in one posture for more than a few seconds. The pup's resilient fat usually enables him to endure the brief pressure of his stepfather's bulky body.

Steller saw love where there was no love: "The parents love their young exceedingly. The females, after parturition, lie in crowds upon the shore with their pups and spend much time in sleeping. The pups, however, directly in the first days play together like children, and imitate their parents in playing at copulation, and practice fighting until one throws the other to the ground. When the father sees this, he rises up with a growl and hastens to separate the combatants, kisses the victor, licks him with his tongue, tries with his mouth to throw him upon the ground, and makes vigorous demonstration of his love for the youngster, who struggles bravely against it. In short, he rejoices that he has a son worthy of himself. But they are less fond of the lazy and ease-loving pups. Hence some of the young are always near the father; others near the mother . . ." It is impossible now even to guess what seal actions led Steller to indulge in flights of fancy so contrary to the realities of sea bear family life.

For the pup's sake—that as a little land animal he may be born on his proper element—the whole fur seal clan has come ashore. Yet from the moment of birth the seal pup is on his own. As if to compensate for parental indifference, the youngsters seek each other's company and travel in pods or groups like their older brothers.

The mother sea otter trains her baby for aquatic life. A fur seal pup has no teacher. Venturing from their birth rocks to the tidal pools, the youngsters paddle about happily. Grown stronger and bolder, they try their luck in the sea. Tossed roughly shoreward by incoming waves, they never grow discouraged. Chattering, snarling at the surf, they launch themselves again and again until they ride through the breakers and remain afloat. When they have learned to swim steadily, they practice more artistic strokes, breaching like dolphins. By autumn they are at home in the water. When they come ashore, they still ramble in pods; their games but mimicry of future adult duties.

By early autumn they have shed their black coats for thicker dark-gray pelts. Having suckled for the last time, like their elders they obey the ancestral edict and set out for warmer latitudes; some not to return home or to land on any shore for a year or two. They must, from the moment of departure, secure their own food. About half of each season's young die during their first winter at sea, either because they cannot secure enough fish, because they lack the strength to swim on and on in turbulent seas, or because they cannot escape killer whales.

The male seal enjoys a boyhood of six seasons; the female may be mated, often by an idle bull, in her second summer. For the rest of her life, she is, except for yearly respites of a few days, gravid, even while nursing her newborn. Normally that respite from gestation varies from 3 to 7 days. Although complete healing of the placental site requires about 6 weeks, one branch of her two-horned uterus can accommodate the initial, slow germination of a new fetus before the other has recovered from the damages of labor. Only one or two instances of a barren cow have ever been detected; none of multiple birth, a circumstance due, probably, to the structure of her uterus and the long period—nearly a year—required for gestation. At the close of the brief postnatal interlude—its duration determined, it seems, by the awakening of her own mating desires—the cow is wooed by her harem lord, affectionately, gently, and quickly. As soon as the bull has served a cow, his tenderness vanishes. Their mutual duty successfully performed, manifold responsibilities claim the bull's attention. The cow slips back abruptly to her old position in the harems, the downtrodden victim, the target of masculine temper and abuse. Pathetic and fleeting is her annual romance.

Toward the end of June, Steller turned to those majestic creatures of the North Pacific, afterward appropriately named Steller sea lions. He reported: ". . . the sea lions live among them in great herds and are much feared by them. They always have the best places. The sea bears do not like to stir up quarrels when the sea lions are present for fear they have of these savage beasts as umpires; for they run up immediately, as I have sometimes seen. So also they dare not try to prevent their females from playing with the sea lions." Contrary to Steller's interpretation of their actions, they are good neighbors, each species tending to its own affairs. Correctly, however, he discerned that, morphologically, the sea bears were more closely related to the sea lions than to ordinary seals: that the two former belonged to an animal class known as the Otariidae, "eared" seals; the latter to the group called the "earless" seals.

By midsummer, as the mating sea beasts began to disperse, the rescue vessel was completed. Again Steller faced an obdurate commander whose first concern was bringing his boat and crew safe to port. Ten *poods* (360 pounds) of luggage Steller could take with him and no more. So he took with him only his manuscripts, a few handfuls of seeds gathered on the brief stop ashore in America and on Bering Island, and a single pair of the curious bony palatal plates, the sea cow's substitute for teeth, and, since even naturalists must provide for an uncertain future, a number of sea otter skins. Otter fur was saleable; a sea bear pelt merely a museum curio.

The formal presentation of *Ursus marinus,* the sea bear, took place in 1751, a decade after Steller and the sea beasts met. Accorded the pomp and dignity of Latin prose, sponsored by the Imperial Russian Academy of Science, the fur seal appeared in the pages of *De Bestiis Marinis.* The author of its life story was unable to receive the congratulations of Europe's excited scholars. Hurrying from Siberia to St. Petersburg in 1747 to answer undeserved charges of misconduct, Steller was taken ill and died, but not before he ended the long masquerade. The sea bear need suffer no longer the obloquy of a borrowed name.

But no single pronouncement of fact was to erase the error of centuries. Linnaeus or one of his disciples surveyed Steller's evidence. A sea animal like a bear? The creature was supposed to resemble the ordinary seal. Despite Steller's proof of indubitable differences between the two mammals, cautious taxonomists compromised and enrolled the sea bear on the roster of *Systema Naturae* as *phoca ursina,* the bearlike seal.

Before the old injustice could be righted in daily speech, Commerce recognized the animal. Seal, sea cat, or sea bear, there was a price on the animal's head, and, as cat or *kotick,* kitten, it became a bookkeeping entry. Russians might say "sea bear" as they chatted, but the first nickname was forever registered in their ledgers. As the fur seal which had hidden so long unmolested under another animal's name became the target of hunters throughout its entire realm, in the seas of the north and the south, a special sealing jargon developed in many languages, especially Russian and English, a miscellany of homely terms borrowed chiefly from the nomenclature of domestic land animals or from the speech of fishermen. And, despite Steller's efforts, the fur seal is still called "sea cat" in Russian, "seal" in most other languages.

4

The Furred Robot

Fur seals of both genera are polygamous, gregarious, and, except for a few subspecies of the Antarctic family, migratory pelagic-littoral mammals. Both the fur seal and the true or earless seal are carnivorous or fish eating and adapted to sea life. Creatures of uneven, divergent evolutionary development, undoubtedly descended from separate extinct prototypes, they are not only dissimilar in appearance and anatomy, but more conspicuously so in degree of intelligence and disposition. Most pronounced are their differences in living habits and mode of locomotion. Shackled by ancient ancestral conventions, the fur seal is merely an animal robot, its every activity monotonously regulated to accomplish the procreation of its kind.

"These married ones are fattest of all," observed Steller, "and without the females they come first to the island, like scouts. All the males have a strong odor, but theirs is the worst. These old animals are very cross and very savage. [Only while breeding.] They live a whole month in one place without food or drink . . ."

Toward the end of April, to their quiet, empty northern beaches—the rock surfaces polished by the beating flippers of innumerable generations—the great bull seals come homing, one by one, from their ocean pastures. Each weighing a quarter of a ton or more, their heavy sooty-brown pelts stretched taut over the thick winter layer of blubber, they haul out to select

25

a plot of rock for their summer's stay. Conflict, deadly in appearance, commences as rivals vie for the most advantageous harem sites. Males stationed nearest the sea will secure the most females. Yet these early squabbles are really halfhearted, mere bluff and bluster. The clash of writhing bodies, the clouds of murky steam curling from wide-opened, sharp-toothed jaws, accompanied by deafening clamor, seems a horrendous exhibition of feral anger. Actually, a bull returning from a cooling sea bath to find another installed in his location, after cursing vigorously in an awesome medley of barks, roars, groans, and whistles, and leaping about aggressively, sidles off warily to find a new home. Or the usurper, after an imposing pretense of resistance, bolts off meekly. This sham warfare does not become bitter, bloody combat until the gravid cows pull their weary bodies from the waves, expel their burdensome infants within a day or two, and come into heat. Their rutting ardor transforms the beachmasters into lustful jealous maniacs, fighting in deadly earnest to protect their females.

Once the cows have arrived, the bulls are sentenced by implacable instinct to imprisonment on their home sites. Invisible boundaries, recognizable only to the animals, restrain them as effectually as solid walls. The female is held prisoner until her infant is born and she has again become pregnant. Then the bull releases her to a nominal freedom, a new drudgery. To nurse her pup, she must travel back and forth between her feeding grounds and breeding beach—a one-way journey for the Pribilof Island cow of 200 miles or more, to areas where squid and fish abound. The Pribilof mother returns from her first postnatal feeding in approximately 2 days, having made a round-trip journey of 300 miles. As her infant grows, he is able to wait longer between nursings, until, as the time for weaning approaches, he is fed only at 5-day intervals. This elastic feeding schedule eases the cow's physical burdens as she provides nourishment for herself, her living pup, and the new life quickening within her.

Along with the first incoming cows, the silver-colored, velvet-fleeced males, not yet seven years old or mature enough to mate, commence to arrive. Adult bulls permit no infertile adolescents to enter their harems. The young upstart, who accidentally crosses forbidden borders, courts injury and death from his older male relatives. Unable to endure solitude, banded together in pods, the bachelors lodge on rocky plots situated haphazardly between and behind the harems. At will they pass back and forth to sea along crooked routes between the breeding seals, dangerous thoroughfares guarded by snarling, suspicious oldsters.

Beachmasters keep sleepless watch, day and night for six to eight weeks, living on the energy of their stored fat. Their pelts begin to hang loosely and clumsily from their frames. Their summer duty performed, they abandon their stations to seek food and refreshment at sea. Whenever they come ashore they loaf in quiet nooks. The beachmaster's domination is over —for that summer. And the fierce-miened bulls are become timorous, weary creatures who scuttle toward the sea when they glimpse an intruder.

As the mating season closes, the rigid divisions of the rookeries vanish. Fur seals of all ages spread out along the coast. They frequent the sandy beaches they shunned earlier and ramble inland to nap on the grass. Until it is time to migrate, the whole seal colony wanders freely in and out of the sea.

The rookery battleground fascinated Steller: ". . . and from a single attack so many duels originate that oftentimes for 2 or 3 furlongs by the seashore you can see nothing but duels, battles, and a thousand sights absurd but bloody, accompanied by a terrific roaring and growling . . . While two often fight for an hour, they make a truce, and both lie down near one another, panting to get their breath. When they are recovered, they both get up and in gladiatorial fashion take a certain place and refuse to leave it as long as the fighting continues. They duck their heads and strike back and one tries to ward off the blows of the other. As long as they are evenly matched, they strike only with their front flippers, but as soon as one gets the advantage of his adversary, he tears him with his teeth and jaws, shakes him, and throws him down. Then the others, who have meantime been mere spectators, seeing this, hurry up to assist the weaker one, as if they were umpires in the fight. With their teeth they inflict wounds as large and cruel as if they were made with a saber. At the end of July a sea bear is seldom seen that is not marked with a wound."

Bulls feel no sporting desire to help a weaker contestant. They rush to watch or join their neighbors' frays only to protect their own harems. Male fighting technique is offensive and defensive. Each attacker strives to rip off his opponent's foreflipper, an always fatal severance. Fighters, lunging at each other's foreflippers, keep their own pressed tightly to their bodies. Consequently, teeth generally miss the target and sink into soft tissues above or below it. With teeth embedded in each other's fat, two embattled males may remain gruesomely clinched until they need air. Again and again, after brief pauses, they repeat this identical thrusting and biting until one tires, weakens, and slinks away or, occasionally, dies. Seldom do a bull's teeth penetrate deeper than his rival's blubber to injure a vital organ. Since the fatty tissue is copiously netted with blood vessels, blood streams from wounds that are not deep or serious, but, because seal blood clots extremely quickly, is soon stanched.

The bulls' determination, at mating time, to remain on their rock stations or die, overawed Steller. He dared not approach one until he had maimed it, even though he noted:

"The very large old ones never run away from a man or a crowd of men, but prepare at once for battle. Nevertheless, I have seen whole herds put to flight if a man whistle. The females flee in haste, and likewise whole droves of adult males, even many thousands are driven in headlong flight to the sea if, suddenly, when they feel secure, they are attacked with a great noise."

He admired his bears at sea: "They swim so rapidly that in an hour they can easily swim two German miles. If they are wounded at sea with a harpoon, they draw the boat with the hunter after them so swiftly that the boat seems to fly, and they often overturn the boat and drown the hunter . . . ," a yarn he must have heard in Kamchatka, where primitive hunters in clumsy boats hated to tangle with *sipang,* the devil, as they called the bull seal. No dexterous American aboriginal hunter knew such dread.

Steller also marveled at their agility on land: "When they climb a rock, they take hold of it with their front flippers as seals do, and drag the rest of their body behind them, bending the back like a bow and holding the head low, to give elasticity to the body. In swiftness they almost if not quite excel the swiftest runner, and the females are especially fast. [The female was dubbed by hunters in the Southern Hemisphere, a "clapmatch."] There is no doubt that many of us would have been killed by them if their legs were worth as much on land as they are in water."

Although fur seekers were soon to learn to kill fur seals easily with a single well-placed blow on the head, Steller and his companions had nearly as bad a time with their sea bears as the De Nodals with the sea lions in the harbor of the Plate. "Those that we first blinded on land with stones," he noted, "were afterward dispatched with clubs without any artifice. But the beasts are so tenacious of life that two or three men beating only their heads with clubs could scarcely kill them with two hundred blows, and frequently would have to rest and refresh themselves two or three times. When the cranium [the fur seal has an unusually thin skull] is broken into little bits and almost all the brains have gushed out, and all the teeth have been broken, he still attacks them with his flippers and keeps on fighting. I have purposely broken the skull and put out the eyes of one and then left him, and afterwards for more than two weeks he still stood alive and unmoved, like a statue, in the same place."

That tragically mutilated, sightless, statuesque bull seal illustrates most poignantly the sea bears' fatal bondage to accursed and hoary impulsions which make them furred automatons, deaf and blind to all change in their ambience, mechanical, ritualistic—and vulnerable.

5

The Fur Seal as an Empire Builder

Tardily the Russians acknowledged the fur seal's share in building their North Pacific empire. Its drabber fur eclipsed by the sea otter's lustrous black velvet wrap, the fur seal possessed the virtues of a drudge: reliability and procurability. Only its usefulness as a marketable fur and a regular source of colonial food and clothing enabled the Russians to remain in America. The sea otter was the prize that beckoned fur seekers through northern seaways; the fur seal, the servant of empire builders.

Russian fortune hunters became acquainted with both sea creatures around the beginning of the 18th century. The Irkutsk merchant Atlasov, the first Siberian to cross the Kamchatkan wilderness to the Pacific's rim, prince of the fierce Kamchadals by adoption, stormed at the head of his aboriginal raiders down to Cape Lopatka at the tip of the peninsula. There he met the sea beaver, as the Russians called it, a fur to challenge sable and ermine. In 1701, when Atlasov knelt before Peter the Great to present 3,500 magnificent furs, the *yassak,* tribute, wrung from the Kamchadals, only 10 were sea otter pelts—sufficient to rouse new fur hungers. Until Empress Catherine abolished the monopoly in 1789, all furs belonged to the Crown. Reimbursing their merchants and hunters well but not richly, the

Czars reaped enormous profits from furs sold in Persia, Turkey, and China. A subject bringing a new fur to Court was welcomed and rewarded.

To curry favor with a monarch notably curious about foreign places and people, Atlasov introduced the shipwrecked sailor, Denbei, he had rescued from the Kamchadals. The first Japanese that the Russians had seen, Denbei, later baptized as Gabriel, revealed to Peter the existence of islands southeast of Kamchatka: the Kurils and Japan.

His role of trail blazer to new hunting grounds played out, Atlasov returned to Kamchatka. Driven by insatiable lust for power and riches, his career of murder and rapine continued there until he was murdered in 1712.

In the year of his death, an inspector from the impatient, fur-conscious Court arrived in Kamchatka to hasten the search for the islands Denbei had described. The sole volunteer was a brutal Polish religious maniac named Kosyrevsky, an inmate of the Yakutsk prison, willing to risk the dangers of an uncharted sea in exchange for his freedom. Released from irons, Kosyrevsky and his henchmen built two crude, unseaworthy boats and reached the two most northerly Kurils. There, accompanying his robberies with elaborate religious thanksgiving services, he stripped the inhabitants of all their furs, but, appropriately, no sooner had he landed in Kamchatka than a shipmate disappeared with his booty.

The revelation of the sea otter's Kuril asylums coincided with an increasing difficulty in finding land fur-bearing animals too ruthlessly hunted down for decades. So, back and forth along the Kuril sea route, charted but still dangerous for their crude boats, unemployed Siberian hunters, with neither royal mandate nor permission, went trafficking clandestinely for otter furs, usually wresting them from the Kurils' "shaggy" Ainus, so much easier to handle than Kamchadal warriors, instead of hunting them. Sea bear skins would induce no hunter to make such dangerous voyages, but the high prices otter furs fetched were paid in gold rubles.

In 1741 Bering's shipwreck accidentally exposed the fur resources of the North Pacific. The survivors' indifference toward the animals which had nourished and strengthened them for their daring attempt to return home, prophetically and mistakenly established the fur seal's reputation in Russian America as a nonentity, useful only in an emergency. Not even Steller would sacrifice a few ounces of his baggage allowance to bring back a single sealskin to illustrate his studies. In Russia, at the time, there existed no market for these skins with the thick guard hairs. In China, where a pelt would sell for a few kopeks, the thick hair was shaved off, and the tough hides tanned and made into durable luggage containers. The survivors' discrimination was richly rewarded. The otter skins they carried back to Siberia sold for $30,000. For the same number of sealskins they would probably not have received 300 rubles.

Those otter furs electrified Siberia. Mysteriously, the report of their arrival was borne to the most remote hunting posts. From tundra and taiga the fur hunters, the *promyshlenniki*, streamed, making for the Kamchatkan port of Petropavlovsk, eager to exchange marked wilderness trails for uncharted waters which led, if the winds favored them, to otter haunts and riches. Impatient merchants, pondering risks, estimating profits, were waiting to employ them. The very next summer a crew set out in a ridiculously small boat called a *shitik* (literally, sewn, because its wooden planks were lashed together with cord, animal thongs, and osier withes). Other hunting gangs in similar crude craft soon followed. Calked with moss and pitch, these cockleshells rode the waves toward Alaska. Not content with the fur yield of the Commander beaches, the hunters ventured beyond, facing the strong winds from America. By 1745 they had reached the islands at the tip of the Aleutian Archipelago. From that date the search was ever eastward until the mainland blocked their way. No one kept track of the sailings or the number of ships which never returned. Russian subjects required official permission to leave their home ports, so unauthorized hunting parties avoided publicity. The Czar rewarded successful disobedience. Lest he punish the disobedient who failed, secrecy was so carefully maintained that knowledge of the earliest voyages is most fragmentary. Forty vessels were hunting back and forth before 1795; the success of their forays soon apparent. Incessant killing quickly exhausted each new hunting ground, and the seekers were forced to push on eastward to get a catch.

Vessels which first visited Bering Island and its neighbor, Copper Island, brought back otter and fox pelts, many cargoes worth more than a million dollars in today's currency. Emilian Bassov, commanding the *Kapitan,* pioneer hunting vessel to make Bering Island in 1743, revisited the Commander Group several times within the following decades. He brought back the first recorded load of sealskins, two thousand of them, in 1746, either as an experiment or, because otter and fox were scarce, to avoid losing money. Merchants grumbled at small profits, but their investments were trifling. The hunters earned small pay for their catch, usually augmented by extra furs they took to sell for themselves. Expected to get their own meat, even when heading for the Aleutian Islands, fur seekers wintered on Bering Island to stock sea cow meat, their favorite marine animal flesh, for their voyage. By 1763 their butchery had emptied the Bering Island larder.

On the uninhabited Commander Islands the hunters killed and skinned the fur-bearing animals themselves, but, after 1745, on the populated islands of the Aleutian Archipelago the *promyshlenniki* exercised their civilized right to collect *yassak* and forced the male villagers to hunt for them. None of the freebooters thought of settlement, of colonization; only of seizing wealth quickly.

The merchants and the Czar amassed wealth. A retired *promyshlennik* was a phenomenon unknown in Siberia. Back from a long voyage, drinking and gambling soon wiped out their earnings. Then, in debt to their trader, they set out in the next ship to America. The fur lust burned in their vitals and drove them to unspeakable crimes, but their shares of profit never secured them comfort or ease. The mirage of richer hunting grounds, the golden shadow of the sea otter, kept them questing. Their lifelong fortitude was the bravery of madness. The merchants first scented a change. Their ships no longer returned at the summer's end, not even at the close of the next year. Vessels delayed from three to seven years in that strange hostile land to the east were more than a merchant's heart could endure, especially when their hunters brought back disappointing cargoes of fox and sealskins. Only sea otter pelts for Chinese mandarins meant wealth. The hunters could afford dreams of new kelp beds, islands just beyond the horizon where fur lay on the beach for the gathering, but the trader, poring over his ledgers, wanted goods and cash. One merchant decided to investigate the hunters' excuses for delay himself.

Gregory Shelekov, Irkutsk trader, shareholder in several small fur companies, including the most successful, Lebedev-Lastochkin, was fired by more than a dream of higher profits. If the New World proved suitable, his secret ambition was to colonize and develop it. To succeed, he must be independent when he reached America so, with two partners, he organized a new company and outfitted three ships. If there were furs, he intended to bring them back to buy the Czar's permit to transform his dream into reality. He sailed with his wife, Natalia, pioneer Russian woman to visit America, aboard the *Three Saints,* August 16, 1783, and wintered on Bering Island. The next season he explored the Archipelago, and eventually anchored in a Kodiak Island bay. The wooded island seemed good for his purpose. But the native Koniags, whom the Russians inaccurately called Aleuts, were hostile. Rejecting Shelekov's friendliest overtures, most of the population retreated to a high, isolated offshore rock. An empire builder has no time to woo subjects. Shelekov sailed the *Three Saints* close to their asylum and called on them to surrender. They refused. His cannon soon cleared the rocky bastion. From those who fell or jumped into the sea or escaped the cannonading, he selected hostages to insure lasting tractability. Shelekov saw that the

New World, so vast and strange and very empty, was aloof, but not wholly inimical. There were furs and fish and other game, fertile soil, and timber for building, and countless treasures still undiscovered. Not far in the future Shelekov pictured a great city on the shore of the harbor he named Three Saints Bay after his ship. Before he left Kodiak, offices, storehouses, and living quarters had been erected. For the first time in the New World the Russians had not burrowed underground in the Stone Age fashion of the aborigines. Bringing with them only alcohol, flour, tobacco, and firearms, the last guarded jealously for themselves alone, they had adopted Aleut dress, food, and shelter, even Aleut hunting methods.

To uphold his claim to Kodiak, Shelekov left in his new village a small group under the command of *Peredovchik* (Chief Hunter) Samilov. He took back many fur seal pelts. A practical man intent on building an empire overlooked no source of income. Cheap or not, they were trade goods, and enough silver kopeks put together added up to a golden ruble. The fur seal was gaining on its rival.

Shelekov, pausing in Irkutsk to pick up his partner Golikov, bore his report and his ambitious scheme to the Empress and a magnificent cloak of black fox skins. His maps and descriptions of America were the first detailed information she had received of her American possessions. Statecraft and feminine pleasure—the voluptuous fox wrap must have delighted Catherine's sensuous nature—made her most gracious to Shelekov's suit. Honors, exclusive hunting rights on Kodiak Island, and the government of his infant colony she granted him—a mere bagatelle compared to the concessions he asked for. One small island out of the great immensity which was Russian America was only a starting-off place.

The Empress was excited by his reports and plans, pained by his revelations of the *promyshlenniki's* barbaric treatment of her new American subjects, and extremely disturbed by details of the visit of the English expedition under Captain Cook to her domain in 1778. Eventually she commissioned the Billings

Expedition to procure an objective picture of life in her new realm. The Empress and Shelekov were both dead when Billings' report reached St. Petersburg, but its conclusions advanced Shelekov's dream for his family and partners.

Kodiak, at least, his own, Shelekov sought a manager for his colony, a man capable of understanding his purpose, ruthless but imaginative, ambitious but devoid of petty self-interest. By one of those historical coincidences that, in retrospect, seem predestined, the man Shelekov needed was available. A middle-aged trader whose post on the Anadyr had just been burned by the Chukchi, a newly made bankrupt, seemed hardly the candidate. But Alexander Baranov was only temporarily bested by adversity. He understood Shelekov's contradictory urges to build an empire and secure millions of furs for personal enrichment. He could read between the lines of Shelekov's letters. For many years, under insuperably difficult conditions, he sent the desired furs to Siberia, held the wild country he called "Rioting Alaska" and its peoples to his purpose, and outfoxed intrusive English-speaking traders. He founded Shelekov's city in southeastern Alaska, a New Archangel, with a cathedral and governor's castle, imposing edifices even though built of logs. He had two allies, the Aleuts and the fur seals, workmen and capital. Had either been lacking, Baranov would have failed.

6

The Fur Seal
Enslaves a People

For generations, tribes of sea hunters had lived on the bleak shores of the Aleutian Archipelago. How many waves of immigration had washed over the islands is unknown, although traces of at least two separate peoples have been uncovered. Legends of the Unangan, who inhabit the islands nearest the Alaska Peninsula, tell that the giant race, *shuganan,* or the First People, were wiped out by flood for their transgressions. Archeological sappers, rooting in buried village sites and violating cavern tombs to measure mummy skeletons, confirm the residence of a tall people. One anthropologist believes they were still occupying some islands when the Russians came. To the conquerors, the difference between a hunter of the Nearer Islands, a Nig'ug of Atka and the other Andreanov Isles, an Unangaq of the Fox Island, or a Koniag of Kodiak, was unimportant. They were all Americans at first, then Aleuts. The immigrants had come from Asia, either across a vanished land bridge far north of the Archipelago or by boat across Bering Strait. Following Alaska's coast southward, they had been diverted, probably by hostile mainland tribes, westward again to settle the islands. Their dialects link them with the Eskimos, at least closely enough to indicate a common ancestral stock. Artifacts in excavated middens reveal that, no matter how many

newcomers drifted in to share the residents' precarious foot-
hold, the culture remained static at the highest level of Stone
Age progress. The islanders remained dependent on the sea's
bounty—the rhythm of their lives timed to the habits of marine
mammals. They used the land almost as the fur seals do—for
breeding only. The men were sons of the sea, physically molded
by the hours they spent with their mother. Apart from their
canoes, waddling clumsily as they walked, they were ungainly.
At sea the man and the boat became a single entity at home in
its genetic element.

To maintain their hazardous lodgment on land, they looked
always to the sea and its creatures, fish and fowl, whale and
walrus, sea lion and otter, fur seal and hair seal, to provide
them food, clothing, heat, light, weapons, material for boats
and shelters. Ashore were sand and rocks to burrow in, sweet
water for their thirst, caverns to entomb their dead. The soil
yielded a sparse harvest of tuberous roots and herbs; dull-
savored berries from low, matted bushes; and grasses for baskets, house mats, and grave wrappings. From the earth's surface they picked up flint, sulfur, rocks for utensils and weapons,
and pumice for burnishing their stone artifacts. There they
found ocher for dyes, hematite for amulets, pebbles for orna-
ments. On land they collected bird eggs, hunted wild fowl,
trapped foxes too ill-flavored for eating save in famine time, and
caught salmon in their streams at spawning time.

Where sea and land clashed on the tidal flats, the waves left
gifts, driftwood from other coasts—too little for fuel, barely
enough for boat frames and house rafters, and their chief building timber, whalebone. The shore offered them mollusks—
clams, oysters, mussels, and the delicate roe of the sea urchin
—crabs and other crustaceans, and sea greens to eat cooked
or raw.

Neither land nor sea gave sustenance lightly and freely. The
islanders lived on the doorstep of extinction, preserved only by
their ceaseless drudgery. A brief holiday from the sea chase
unleashed famine. All toiled. Women, children, and the old dug

roots, gathered eggs and shellfish, caught and dried salmon, picked berries and stored them dried or in fat, cleaned the game and flensed the skins, boiled the blubber and stored it in animal bladders, plucked the grasses and dried them for winter weaving. The women repaired boat skins and clothing, tanned hides and prepared animal membranes for waterproof garments, sorted and dyed bird feathers, tended to their semi-underground houses and their children.

Weather-bound, the men manufactured tools, utensils, and weapons from bone and stone; objects often beautiful, smoothly polished, carved, and decorated. The women had their eternal sewing and grass weaving. There was time for games and dancing; time for stories and poetry and the endless preachments of old men whom the young must never offend by display of boredom. In those underground refuges from the wind, there must have been laughter and happiness as the men's knives traced patterns on ivory and the women's fingers twisted fine grass slivers into intricate designs. Their ancient songs—only eleven were preserved—are the songs of a stoical, not a morbid, people.

Their daily lives were governed, not by their creator deity—his work ended when he had made and peopled their world—but by a host of good and evil spirits and, especially, the personalized vindicative elements, a logical belief in view of their lives. After death, as invisible kindly protectors of their living kin, the islanders expected to linger near their homes. In midwinter, perhaps to mark the closing year, men and women, naked save for tall, stark, unpainted driftwood masks, danced back to back in parallel lines in the bitter night wind. To lift a dancer's mask was sacrilege punishable by instant death. A man possessed by an evil spirit, the shaman or *qugag'iq,* was the village pariah, supposed, by chant and drumbeat incantations, to cure the sick, secure good hunting, and calm storms endangering hunters out at sea. From the vital rites of marriage, birth, death, and sacrifices, he was barred.

So little is known of their religion, because the old men were dead and the young men remembered little to tell their first true friend, the missionary Veniaminov, in 1825, and his records suffer, also, from his religious bent. Aleut ethics, preserved chiefly by him, reflected a pragmatic philosophy. Be good to the poor lest the role of rich and poor be reversed by fortune. Be kind to the old because all grow old. Be kind to the stranger and guest that he may spread a good report abroad.

Islanders owned slaves, prisoners taken when they attacked their villages. Penalties that slaves suffered for disobedience, like those of medieval Europe, consisted of body mutilation. The Aleuts, it seems, went warring only in retaliation against their most persistent raiders, the Koniags.

Their dead were eviscerated; the intestines, cleaned and stuffed with sweet-scented grasses, were reinserted into the abdomen. The body, folded in the favorite resting posture of the living, squatting on their heels with their knees touching their chests, were wrapped in several layers of woven grass cerements. Food and the trappings of daily life were placed beside the mummy.

The Aleuts, according to relics found in graves and garbage pits, loved beauty and wove it into their baskets, dyed it into their garments, and chiseled it on bone, ivory, and stone. They wrought decorations out of pebbles and shells and wore labrets in their lips and necklaces of animal teeth. They wore dyed feathers and painted their faces. Their poems reveal their sensitivity. Hardy and dauntless, they were a kindly, friendly people, as the Russians saw when the keels of their boats crunched on the shingles of new islands and unarmed inhabitants came toward them, making friendly gestures. But, that day in 1745 when Nevodchikov and Chuprov landed on Attu, a cataclysm more violent than nature could wreak struck the islands and their inhabitants.

The Attu Islanders greeted that landing party reverently as benign, bearded gods come in a gigantic boat from the west as an ancient *qugag'iq* had foretold, kneeling to receive their holy visitors. Conducted to their *ulux,* the Russians, stung with hot avarice at the sight of furs, fell on their hosts savagely. Leaving dead and wounded hunters, violated women, and homes stripped bare of furs behind them, they went on to raid the thirty-one settlements on nearby Aggatu.

A gang led by seaman Belayev began the attack, seizing the boats along the shore to cut off their victims' one road of escape. The men and aged they met, they killed, sparing but one boy to train as interpreter. Some women were spared; others raped and murdered, their lifeless, still warm bodies flung over the cliffs. Then the raiders collected all furs and food. Commander Chuprov, even more vicious than Belayev, liked to see a man crumple under the impact of his iron club. Aboard his ship, he fed captives gruel mixed with corrosive sublimate to enjoy their slower death agonies.

Not all Russian hunters were diabolical sadistics. The reputation of Trepeznikov, who explored the Andreanov group after 1750, is stainless. Only from necessity did his navigator, Nakvashin, carry off an Atkan lad to educate as interpreter. But for every Trepeznikov there were a dozen or more Belayevs or Chuprovs. When survivors sent word to the east that madmen were on their way, islanders armed with club and spear were defenseless against firearms. Siberian hunters stripped furs, not from animal carcasses, but from the bodies of slain Aleuts, and from their beds and walls and drying frames, until the effects of their razing struck home to them. New or returning hunters found no dried furs ready to load aboard. The *promyshlenniki* would have to chase the sea otter to its favorite perilous waters. The islanders' seamanship saved them from extinction, not by carrying them to safer coasts beyond the newcomers' grasp but by enabling them to exchange their lives for fur-hunting services. Only their lives they bought—and dearly. The *promyshlenniki* took every pelt as tribute. Masters waited on by the household, they camped in their vassals' homes, keeping warm, drinking and gambling. Physically, they lived the life of the Stone Age people. Spiritually they inhabited a foul abyss; their brutal conduct incomprehensible to the neolithic-minded primitives. The swaggering fur corsairs took the complete subjugation of their hunting slaves for granted, but, after nearly twenty years of persecution, the Aleuts revolted.

The first blow was struck when Captain Bashmakov's vessel *Jeremiah* was wrecked off Adaq. Taking advantage of their oppressors' misfortune, the inhabitants rushed out to drive the survivors, scrambling toward land, back into the sea. They killed only one Russian and wounded another. Infuriated and outraged by twofold disaster, the *promyshlenniki* charged ashore and beat off the attack. The two years they waited for another ship were one long castigation of the rebels.

Bashmakov, opposed when he tried to land at Kiska and Tanaga, foiled a villagers' uprising on the latter. To teach the rebels to desist, when two men came to bargain for the release of a small boy captive—the lad's father and a friend—Bashmakov staked them out on deck. Boiling tar was poured over them before they were finally beheaded. Then, after all furs had been removed, the Russians burned the huts. The boy prisoner, sent to Kamchatka and baptized as Ivan, is reported to have become a Cossack.

Captain Glotov won many friends among Unimak and Unalaska Aleuts and persuaded a chief's son, at least, to be baptized. Several years later, news reached him on Kodiak Island that his old friends had beguiled a shipload of *promyshlenniki* with strong drink at a feast and murdered all but four. Back he sailed, a deadly avenger storming from village to village; in his wake, bleaching bones and ashes. New Russian arrivals joined the crusade of vengeance that historians euphemistically labeled "the Period of Pacification." There were Russian names that generations of Aleuts remembered, none more bitterly than Soloviev, the Terrible Nightingale, notorious for cruel sport in peace, crueler savagery in war. Tying Aleuts one behind another to see how many bodies a single bullet could penetrate—nine, it is alleged—had been a nursery game compared to the abominable penalties he devised to subjugate the rebels.

For twenty years the uneven struggle continued until the

islanders were beaten. Once more the *promyshlenniki* stalked
among the huts, unarmed and secure, while nature blotted out
the reproachful scars. Rain washed the bloody beaches. Grass
flourished in the fertile dust of empty villages. Islands once
ringed with settlements were empty of human life. Not quite
two thousand souls remained of ten times that number, at least,
before 1745. The sea engulfed hundreds fleeing before the paci-
fiers. Few fugitives found haven with other tribes. When their
food providers died, the women, children, and the old succumbed to hunger. The channels of oral tradition blocked by
death, tribal culture, history, and art vanished along with the
last spark of confidence in their deities. The islanders' laughter
and their song were stilled. They retained of their past only
their language. Decades later, their conquerors complained of
the Aleuts' melancholy habit of rising at night to sit impassively
for hours gazing at the sea. The stoicism that had braced them
to live on their harsh islands had become fatalism.

There was peace along the Archipelago when Shelekov came
—the peace of slavery, and pliant human toilers to do his will.
And, in the year in which Shelekov bowed before the Empress
to disclose his dream, a rich new mine of Alaskan furs was
opened. The fur seal, itself man's victim, manacled the Aleut
people.

The history of the two, yoked together, has been mutual and
reciprocal ever since 1786. As serfs of Imperial Russia and still
today as American and Soviet citizens, the descendants of those
ancient, independent sea hunters have remained linked by law,
circumstance, or tradition to the fur seal's service.

7

The Fur Seal's Last Northern Stronghold

Generations of Aleut hunters had speared fur seals in the straits between their islands but had never seen one haul ashore. Every spring they speared females, swollen with young, heading northward; every fall the fat little dark-gray pups, their flesh so sweet and tender, were captured swimming south. The Aleuts understood the rhythm of fur seal migrations. To the north, they knew, were uninhabited islands where the fur seals bred. In warmer southern latitudes, they assumed, other islands were the animals' secluded refuge from winter storms. The Aleuts shared no secrets with their hated conquerors. Since the *promyshlenniki* cared for nothing but furs, when the furs were gone, they would go home. The islanders would regain their liberty and peace.

But the *promyshlenniki* had hunters' eyes. They watched the migrating fur seals and pondered their destination. Not traveling toward Copper or Bering Islands, where the beaches after years of killing were almost bare in mating time, these seal voyagers had other hideouts, islands lying in the boisterous sea to the north or in the quieter realm of the Pacific. To trace the fur seal routes in the foggy Bering would be more perilous. Most seal-spying ships sailed blindly back and forth in the broad lonely expanse of the Pacific south of the Archipelago.

Swift-swimming fur seals passed them by, and the mariners cursed and veered from one point of the compass to another. They found no islands. Some captains, more venturesome, headed north; but the Bering's violent squalls always drove them back to the shelter of Aleutian bays. For nearly two decades the fur seals eluded their pursuers.

Then Gerassim Pribylov, a mate serving the Lebedev-Lastochkin Company as Commander of the sloop *St. George,* chose to try his luck in the north. His father, some said, had accompanied Bering. Others claimed he was a peasant's son born with an inexplicable itch for the sea. Whatever his heredity, he was all sailor. Afterward it was said he was no gambler, that an Aleut *qugag'iq,* a wise man of Unalaska, had violated tribal secrecy and had told him the ancient chronicle of Igadik, the daring son of an Unimaq chief. To the shores of an island thronged with fur-bearing animals, winds had blown Igadik's animal-skin *iqaq.* He passed the storm-bound winter hunting. On a miraculously clear spring day, the lonely youth saw to the south the familiar peaks of Unimaq penciled on the sky line. After paddling for four days he came safely home to his father's *uluq,* bearing an incredible number of sea otter tails to prove his account of the fur-bearing host he had met on Amiq. Striving to win fame as a daring sea voyager and hunter, many an Aleut stripling after him must have hunted there. Yet no Russians heard of Amiq, until, if jealous gossip can be trusted, the Unalaskan shaman was won over by Pribylov's friendship or succumbed to a bribe. At a drinking bout in an underground Unalaskan shelter, a tongue, unhinged by *qvass,* may have wagged within Pribylov's hearing—and thereby extended the Russians' stay in America for nearly a century.

Perhaps uninformed but sailing under fortune's star, Pribylov slipped quietly out of the harbor of Iluluq with a crew of Russians and Aleuts on a June day in 1786 and steered north, enviously eying passing fur seals unaffected by the movement of the winds and sure of their destination. Three weeks he sailed, trying to read the flotsam on the waves for a clue to land. On

June 25th fur seal voices guided him through thick fog to the high cliffs of an island. Cautiously he nosed his vessel along the formidable rock ramparts which lined most of the coast. Where the sea walls were broken, furred animals obliterated the shore. Finally a boat ventured to approach the frowning barrier of Tolstoi Mys, the Thick Headland. A sure-footed hunter climbed deftly from one narrow ledge to another and threw down a rope to his companions. Inevitably Pribylov called the island St. George, after his vessel's patron saint. The cliff is still known by its Aleut name, the "Thanking Place." The Aleuts were not grateful that their oppressors had found new hunting grounds. Undoubtedly the Russians christened the site where they planted the Greek cross and prayerfully took possession of the land, and only ironical mischance kept the translation alive as a place name until now.

The *St. George* soon crammed with furs, Pribylov returned to Unalaska's harbor of Iluluq to winter and replenish supplies. Twenty Russians and twenty Aleuts were left on the island under *Peredovchik* Efim Popov to collect more furs. Their absence caused much speculation in Iluluq. News of Pribylov's rich cargo crept from one *uluq* to another. Ships were outfitted, ready to follow him north in the spring.

On St. George his hunters passed busy months trapping foxes and hunting the sea animals that wintered along the shores. Before spring their tea, alcohol, and flour were exhausted. Day succeeded day, and no sail crossed the horizon. The lonely company began to fear that the Bering winds had destroyed Pribylov; that they might be marooned forever among the fur seals. When skies were clear, sentries paced the headlands and surveyed the emptiness of the sea with increasing despair. One bright afternoon a pair of keen eyes, scanning the sea in all directions, came to rest on a shadowy smudge on the northeast sky line. Unmistakable the contour of the mass. Land! Immediately Popov manned their *nidiliq,* the large Aleut skin boat. Eagerly the hunters pushed their craft through the waves; forty miles they paddled furiously. On the holy day of St. Peter and

St. Paul, July 11th by today's reckoning, the prow of the *nidiliq* nosed on the soft sands of the last and greatest of the fur seal's northern strongholds, *Amiq*. Named at once in honor of the two saints, the title, too long and clumsy for constant usage, was soon abbreviated to St. Paul.

The low coast of the new island, larger than St. George, was inviting breeding space to marine fur bearers. Every rocky beach along the forty-mile coast was hidden by its occupants, millions of fur seals, thousands and thousands of sea otters and sea lions. The discoverers landed in a small cove between the wings of two rambling headlands on the western coast, a beach still known as Zapadni, Western. Shoving through the teeming crowd, the hunters started inland. Just beyond the beach, sheltered by the thick stand of tall sea rye or elymus grass, they stumbled on the charred traces of a campfire. Someone had stopped there very briefly and, since the sand had not yet hidden the ashes, not long before them. They sifted the ashes, worried lest rival hunters had already found this treasure island, and dug about in the grass roots for clues to the unknowns' identity. They found only the stem of a clay pipe, a broken tinderbox, and a rusty copper European sword hilt, and could only speculate if the erratic explorer, Joan Synd, had stopped off in 1786, or another hunting party—their vessel destroyed by the perfidious Bering before they could report their discovery.

The Aleuts admitted St. Paul was their Amiq. A half century after the Russians took possession, resident sealers guided Bishop Veniaminov to Igadik's camp site. The legend was undoubtedly historical fact. The Aleuts, their storytelling talents not wholly blunted, invented a farcical tale to blame the Creator of the world for guiding Pribylov to Amiq's fur seals.

In the beginning, when God fashioned the world, from the breast of the sea's floor He had bidden the Pribilof Islands rise. The first land to break through the waves was the double-coroneted crest of Bogoslov, a St. Paul volcano named "Word of God," to mark its prompt obedience to His Word. Then God ordered the fur seals to breed on the islands. English, Dutch,

A Seal Pup Talks Back

Telephoto View of Rookery on Day of Annual Harem Census, St. Paul Island

Spanish—all the nations of the world sought their hiding place and failed because God drew about His prize a thick mantle of fog which the irreligious could not penetrate. When the Russians came seeking furs the fog melted, and God rewarded His most devoutly religious followers. No Aleut ever believed this yarn, but many of their Russian masters accepted its blatant irony as merited praise.

The wonder and astonishment that Popov's men felt on beholding the multitude of living furs did not protect the animals. Pribylov, returning at last with two vessels to take off the skins, found his fur kingdom enlarged, encompassing wealth awesome and incalculable. He could not carry away his spoils. When his first cargo arrived in Siberia in 1789, Shelekov wrote despairingly to Delarov, his Unalaska agent, that Pribylov's 40 hunters had secured in 2 years 2,000 sea otters, 40,000 fur seals, 6,000 blue fox skins, and 1,000 *poods* of walrus ivory. For lack of space they had cached 500 *poods* of whalebone on the new islands. Dissatisfied with his share of Lebedev-Lastochkin's profits, Shelekov did not rebuke Delarov too severely for disobeying his previous instructions to send a ship north, but he wrote, "Do not lose this golden opportunity. Soon the animals will be scared away. Do not delay." Traders, whose agents had been less dilatory, rejoiced over fortunes their captains, who had pursued Pribylov in 1787, brought them. Passing the Popov encampment at Zapadni, a dozen or more groups of *promyshlenniki* and Aleuts settled near other beaches, each jealously guarding its chosen sector.

Year after year they went on killing, recklessly slaying more animals than they could skin. Pelts, staked out to dry, soon covered the island like a continuous tarpaulin. Yet the rock ribs of the beaches were not bared by the absence of so many animals. Not for many seasons. Skins they had no time to stake to dry rotted close to the living animals. Digging into the ground to make shelters like the Aleut *uluq,* the hunters lived in filth. Compared to those burrowing men gone wild with loneliness, greed, and intemperance, the sea lions were conspicuously dignified, the sea otters incredibly dainty and fastidious, and the fur seals extremely placid and mild-tempered. When the hunters staggered, besotted, from their dirty lairs to kill, they were murdering their betters.

Each hunter had a fur quota to fill for his employer. If he took more, they belonged to him. Without a kopek in their pockets, they had inexhaustible gambling funds. On the pleasant curving sickle of Zolotoi Beach on St. Paul, literally the "Golden Sands," they crouched over the rolling dice on the slimy earth floors of their dens. The winner rose from his knees and, from the entrance, pointed out living furs he desired. In a few minutes his hot bloody winnings would be flung at him, and the players bent to their game again. More often red than gray, the golden name the sands earned only translated such bloody coins into rubles. On St. Paul's north shore is Vesolia Mista, the jolly place, where hunters drank themselves into sodden insensibility. Now immortalized in the melodious lullaby of Kipling's "The White Seal," the name of the hunter Lukanon, notorious as torturer and assassin of Aleuts, still clings to the black basalt platform of the beach where he killed five thousand sea otters and many more fur seals in one summer.

Seasons passed, and Pribilof beaches were slowly drained of life. Port records contained only receipts of the less profitable sealskin. For each one unloaded in Kamchatka, a dozen or more spoiled on the killing field. Ignoring their own massacre of furred creatures old and young, male and female, hunters complained that the sly animals had slipped away to lonelier shores, and they must go to sea to ferret out their hiding places. Providence and the winds would lead them once again to fur-clad shores.

The hunters talked much of new islands, the missionary, Archimandrit Joseph, complained to Shelekov, but "they are not discerning them." Mariners volunteered to lead expeditions, but no ship sailed. "They are trying to hide something," insisted Joseph. Even the veteran discoverer Pribylov could not be trusted. When his mastless ship tossed helplessly between

Kodiak and Chugach, all aboard, including two clerks, literate and consequently more credible than uncouth mariners, swore they had seen new land, but Pribylov could not recall its bearings. There were plots afoot to seize new rookeries for themselves or a rival company, Joseph insinuated to discredit a man he hated bitterly, Shelekov's agent Baranov.

Agitated dreaming of new fur islands was futile. Pribylov had stormed the fur seal's last northern fastness but only chance attached his name to his discovery. Untitled seamen might discover land; only officers and aristocrats lent their names to new possessions, so Pribylov had named his islands Subarov for a Russian official. Others, discussing his find, referred to the New Islands, Fur Seal Islands ("Cat Islands" in their tongue), the Northern Islands, but, since his name distinguished them most clearly, spoke so frequently of Pribylov's Islands that map makers made the latter official. Only his misdeeds received further mention from his contemporaries.

Checking fur shipments in Kamchatka, Shelekov heard of shady transactions among hunting crews and blustered at Baranov to police his realm more carefully. Baranov reminded him of the size of Russian America and the nature of the men he commanded. Even Pribylov, he raged, stole furs and sold them to his former employer, to Lebedev-Lastochkin agents. That beast of a drunkard Pribylov had broken into Baranov's personal mail and stolen all the vodka, white brandy, and alcohol sent him by his brother. Moistening his dry lips at the thought of his lost liquor, Baranov wrote on of other colonial matters, then added an explosive postscript: Pribylov had swallowed a whole flask without taking his lips from the bottle—an unbearable affront for a thirsty man to forgive.

Forced by storm to take settlers he was transporting to Yakutat Bay back to Kodiak, in March 1796, Pribylov's last voyage was a failure. A year after that disaster, the old seaman who had given Russia the resource on which to build its colonial empire, died—some said while intoxicated, an impoverished, friendless drunkard branded as a petty thief.

A new chapter of Russian-American history opened in 1799. Shelekov's dream was to be tested. Some traders, forewarned, bought shares in the United American Company, first successor to Shelekov's Company. Dispossessed ones gathered up their dried pelts and sailed for Siberia, many to seek employment in the new company. Lebedev-Lastochkin counted its last shipment of 60,000 sealskins, all, probably, from the islands their first mate had discovered. Only 80 of their 200 employees returned, 2 of their 3 ships had been lost in American waters, but the owners had gleaned many golden rubles from Alaska's beaches, especially from the sea bears' island of Amiq.

8

The Fur Seal as Coin
of the Realm

In the last year of the 18th century, Emperor Paul entrusted his American territory to the Russian-American Company, the outgrowth of Shelekov's Company and its one-year-old successor, the United American Company, for a period of twenty years. Substantial investors were Shelekov's widow, his former partners, and his son-in-law, Chamberlain Rezanov. "To show how useful I find your undertaking . . . ," Paul bought twenty shares of stock for himself and four for his wife, consigning his dividends to charity. Other relatives followed his example. Royal dividends would be high: duty collected at Kiakta on furs going into China, duty paid on the imported tea and cotton cloth for which they were bartered, and for the same Chinese merchandise when it was re-exported to other lands.

The directors imitated their betters, allotting prudently—and publicly—at their first meeting one half of one per cent of each ruble of future dividends to the relief of the poor. In private they formulated their colonial government policies, reducing a great undertaking to a simple scheme to earn high dividends from furs. Too profit-conscious to be colonizers, they were too ignorant of events affecting international fur trading to handle their enlarged fur business capably. They were not aware that the pursuit of the Antarctic seal for its pelts instead of its oil had begun a few seasons before Amiq was discovered, and was, by 1799, a flourishing and important trade link between China and nations bordering both sides of the Atlantic. Most consequential was the fulfillment of Simpson's prophecy after a century's delay.

The sealskin was at last a fur. An ingenious Chinese inventor had found out how to pluck out the stiff guard hairs without damaging the fine underfur. Shrewd Chinese merchants suppressed the circumstances of their new fur industry's beginnings so thoroughly that the name of the inventor and the date of his success have been lost. Undoubtedly seal fur had become popular, even fairly common, before an Okhotsk trader uncovered the Chinese secret in 1797. Perhaps the discovery of the dehairing process preceded and inspired the first Antarctic seal huntings for the Chinese trade. By the time Russian agents at Kiakta asked higher prices for their sealskins, their Chinese customers, no longer dependent on Russian seals, were able to haggle until, grudgingly, in 1799, they agreed to exchange five rubles' worth of tea for a sealskin. With this niggardly advance the Russians, probably not realizing then or even later the extent of the competition which kept the price of their one stable and certain colonial resource so low, had to be content.

Petty traders at heart, the directors planned colonial administration in terms of trivial business minutiae, especially how to keep fur-collecting expenses low. Prohibited from selling furs to anyone else, *promyshlenniki* in Company service must continue to pay their own way, as they had for private trading companies, by selling their employers their furs at the rate of one paper ruble for a sealskin, fifty for an otter pelt. Fifty rubles would tempt a hunter to endure privation hunting otters. A single ruble was recompense enough for killing the harmless, rookery-bound fur seals.

The fur empire was divided into three districts. Until he was appointed chief colonial manager and moved to New Archangel, Baranov ruled from Kodiak to Sitka and as much farther south as he dared venture. Larionov, stationed at Unalaska, was responsible for hunting from Atka to the mainland and on the Pribilofs. The remaining Aleutian Islands, the Kurils and the Commanders, nominally in charge of Ladigin installed on Atka, were actually governed directly by the Okhotsk office which, on at least one occasion, ordered Ladigin to send a large hunting crew to the Pribilofs for fur seals. Instructing these managers to deport unskilled Russian hunters at once and hire Aleuts, paying each native hunter sixty rubles' worth of goods a year, the Russians began to erect their empire on two cornerstones: the fur seals and the Aleuts.

The Company adopted the tactics of the independent *promyshlenniki* who had dragooned Aleut hunters to accompany them on their travels. Proclaiming that they were recruited "voluntarily," they transformed the settled islanders into perpetual transients, migrant hunters, and, at times, warriors. Baranov led them to invade Kolosh territory to found, at Sitka, his colonial capital, New Archangel. Each year, at his bidding, fleets of hundreds of *iqax—baidarki* the Russians called them, hunted the sea otter in southeastern Alaska. From Sitka he dispatched them southward to explore and hunt on coastal land now part of the United States and on the Farallones Islands. Rashly foolhardy was the Aleut hunter who hung back when Russian chiefs summoned him to "volunteer" to wage war, explore, or go on long hunting trips. Colonial agents knew how to interpret the adjective voluntary, so lavishly sprinkled throughout their orders from Russia, to their superiors' satisfaction—and profit.

Before the Russian-American Company took over, in May 1786, Shelekov had instructed Samilov: "All Aleuts from Fox's Islands, who left voluntarily (!) their own homes, and who are staying with us with their women and children, should be given good care. They must be given food, clothing, and foot-wear just as the Russians get. Especially the interpreters, and the most prominent of them should be well-clothed." Samilov should buy only furs Aleuts offered to sell "voluntarily" and refuse iron articles in exchange—to comply with the Czar's prohibitions—even if he lost furs to rival companies. Shelekov's public orders were designed to impress the Czar. He abused Baranov violently on one occasion for failing to read between the lines, a mistake the latter rarely made. At least once Baranov's orders were accompanied by a personal, private instruction to ignore the official ones.

Bands of Aleut sealers were scattered over the northern Pacific, traveling back and forth from one productive hunting island to another, sometimes accompanied by their families, but not because the Russians pitied lonely men. The women mended boats and hunting gear, flensed skins, and performed other drudgery so that the hunters could spend more time tracking down and killing fur-bearing creatures. They followed the course of sealing. If Kuril seals were plentiful, Attu and Rat Island hunters were settled there for one season or several. When word came of a seal increase on Commander beaches, the hunters were hurried off to Copper or Bering Island. On the Commander and the Pribilof Islands settlements gradually became permanent. Displaced Aleuts lived so long on the Commanders, on the Pribilofs, or in Alaskan coastal settlements, that their former villages became alien. In 1867 they exercised their truly voluntary right to remain where they resided, where their descendants still live. Only those stranded on the Kuril Islands demanded to be rescued when Russia gave up those seal islands to Japan.

From the beginning, the Okhotsk office was an inefficient link between the colony and the General Administration in St. Petersburg; the latter too far, psychologically as well as geographically, to be interested in colonial growth. Directors did not echo Shelekov's, "None of this small village stuff." In 1803, pleased though fearful when Baranov shipped furs worth 2½ million rubles, including 280,000 fur seal pelts, the report that a half million more sealskins were held in American storehouses caused the Petersburg gentry to countermand Pribilof sealing lest the market, already falling, be ruined. Since thousands were slashed or damaged by rot, and many were old pelts from Shelekov's time, the directors overestimated their reserve. Most had eventually to be burned.

Baranov cursed Okhotsk inefficiency picturesquely, but his strong language inspired no reforms. Ship sailings were delayed—often for years; useless goods arrived instead of those Baranov pleaded for; furs waiting transportation spoiled. He had to devise means to support his settlements or permit Russian Alaska to fail, a defeat that Baranov could not or would not contemplate.

Each year English and Yankee ships visited the Northwest Coast to buy furs from the Indians. Royal edict prohibited trade, even social intercourse, with foreigners, but Baranov had to deal with these rivals or let his colony starve. He had no funds but he had fur seals. He treated the Pribilof Islands as a bank holding inexhaustible assets, a natural reserve of self-renewing currency.

Knowing adversity forced Baranov to buy from them, foreign traders asked fifty times more than the usual local barter rates for their goods and paid only a few cents for a seal fur. To avert famine, Baranov paid their blackmail prices, wined and dined them in his log "castle," and persuaded them to carry his seal-skins to the Canton market.

His disobedience soon known in Russia, the directors wrote hysterically, forbidding him even to speak to foreigners. More justified in being hysterical in 1802, the directors blamed Alaskan fur export to Canton for destroying their market at Kiakta, where Chinese merchants did not even want to buy their otter pelts. Fur seals were so plentiful and cheap that Baranov could be confident the directors would eventually overlook his using them, but he sent all his valuable otter furs to Russia. In 1802 southern sealskins were shipped to Russia's eastern borders, a new threat to Company profits. Czar Alexander notified his Minister of Commerce to admit no "gray beavers from some Cape Island"; the skins were deported.

Regardless of declining profits—a share of the Company dropped from 500 rubles to 280—until the home office sent him goods he needed, Baranov could not stop his disadvantageous trading, which, on receipt of the comprehensive report of Chamberlain Rezanov, Shelekov's son-in-law, in 1804, the directors authorized him to carry on. The Chamberlain informed the directors that only Baranov's boldness had preserved their venture. Rezanov visited St. Paul Island in 1805. Horrified by the frightful waste of such potential astronomical seal wealth, he enforced orders sent from St. Petersburg in 1803 to cease sealing, and set the Aleuts hunting walrus ivory on nearby Walrus Island.

Baranov continued to feed and clothe his colony with the fur seal's help. Most business schemes he tried out were based on sealskins. In 1807 he sent the *Neva* to the Sandwich (Hawaiian) Islands to exchange sealskins for salt and sandalwood. His last attempt to keep trading sealskins there was frustrated by disobedient employees in 1815. So many of a large shipment of Baranov's seal furs that Captain O'Cain took to Canton were badly cured and rotting he had to sell them for eighty kopeks apiece. Until 1814 Baranov even rented his Aleut hunters to foreign traders, accepting goods in part payment for their services, the rest in furs.

Against sharp Yankee and artful British traders the Russians were ill-matched. Of the three ships, paid for with his fur seal coin, which Baranov bought from those detestable "Republicans from Boston" in 1811, one proved too unseaworthy to make even a single voyage. A Captain Bennet carried fur seals obtained from Baranov to Okhotsk instead of Canton. The bewildered Company agent paid outrageous prices for his cargo to prevent his selling them in China. English skipper Piggot tried the same trick; the Russians ordered him to take his skins elsewhere. When he induced a minor clerk in Kamchatka to pay 15 rubles apiece for skins he had bought for 2½, the Company refused to recognize the purchase and charged the hapless clerk 35,000 rubles for shipping the furs on its vessel from Petropavlovsk to Okhotsk.

The foreigners' worst offense was selling firearms and ammunition to the unfriendly Kolosh and other tribes who used them against Sitka, Yakutat, and Baranov's hunting parties. Because the northward expansion of John Jacob Astor's fur trade was blocked by the English, Astor's agents offered Baranov an alliance which proved brief and costly. Each agreed to respect the other's hunting territories and sell no arms to the Indians. Astor's men were to transport goods to Sitka and collect their pay in furs from distant hunting posts, even the Pribilof Islands. The Astor skipper, Captain Ebbetts, carried sealskins to Canton and charged too much for goods he brought back. Able to buy only half of the overpriced goods Astor's Captain Sol brought him, as usual in a crisis, Baranov fell back on his reliable fur seals and gave the Captain a check on his Pribilof bank for 124,000 rubles' worth of sealskins, which Sol sailed north to cash. Several shipwrecks, the crew of one Astor vessel massacred at Nootka Sound, prevented regular deliveries. When the Russians discovered Astor's men were selling arms secretly to the Indians, Baranov again had to wait for the arrival of chance visitors. While his colony fared badly, the Czar was still collecting a million rubles a year in duty at Kiatka alone. The impasse of 1802 there had been temporary, but the volume of trade was decreasing slightly each year.

To stimulate hunting zeal, the directors doubled the sealskin price except to the Cossack foreman and the Aleut hunters maintained by Baranov on the Farallones Islands off California, to seal and collect bird eggs. The Farallones seals, members of the Antarctic genus, were small animals; their pelts were not so silky or so thickly fleeced as those of their northern relatives, so their sales value was much less, too little to warrant an increase in their hunters' wages.

Concurrent with the raise, the first attempt to manufacture colonial currency was made in Russia, crude parchment stamps made of walrus hides, the very wrappers in which furs had arrived from Alaska.

Before the first charter expired, nearly a million fur seal skins had been exported; but, between 1804 and 1812, another

million, damaged by careless knives or hasty curing with arti-
ficial heat, had been thrown into the sea or burned. Neither age
nor sex restrictions protected the seals. Several times a *zapusk,*
or holiday from killing, was enforced when the rookery populations thinned conspicuously, a rest on one set of islands co-
inciding with the resumption of sealing on another. Fur seals
provided too great a share of essential meat and clothing for
the colony to discontinue sealing on all rookeries at once or for
very long. Dried sea lion and seal flesh was shipped to all stations—from St. Michael on the Yukon to the smallest Aleutian
settlement and down to Sitka. Skins for clothing, and throat
and intestinal membranes for waterproof garments were brazenly included as part of an Aleut's sixty-ruble annual wage.
Attempting to manufacture hats, gloves, and socks from seal
fur, apparently by weaving, Baranov reported he failed because
"the hair being short, the wool was found to be unsatisfactory."

In 1819 the Company's charter was renewed. Baranov, the
daring old man who had kept Russian America alive and ex-
panding and had whipped the raw land to his will, was re-
placed. There were no empire builders to succeed him—only
ordinary mortals. His departure, after twenty-seven years at
the helm, marked the peak of colonial progress. While crossing
the Pacific on his way home, the wonder of Alaska still tugging
at his heartstrings, he died on the Sandwich Islands.

During the term of the second charter, the Company's earnings were reduced by at least a quarter of its former income.
Fur-bearing animals decreased so rapidly that less than a half
million fur seal pelts were secured, the loss only partially offset
by the purchase of beaver pelts from Indians at a new post on
the Kuskokwim River. Governor Muraviev traded sealskins to
foreign traders visiting Sitka for eight years. Then the Pribilof
bank failed. Yankee skippers had to be paid with letters of
credit on the General Administration.

The use of sealskins for casual local barter and as currency
had been an expensive expedient: ridiculously low sealskin barter value versus extortionate trade good prices. Desultory trade

with Spanish California was unprofitable—sealskins exchanged too cheaply for flour. After 1833, when the Farallones hunters took only fifty-four fur seals, the Aleuts were removed from the southern boundary of Russian America. Russia's New World empire was shrinking, each recession dramatically linked to the ebbing flow of fur seal life.

Baron Wrangel, one of Baranov's most capable successors, tried to succor seal life by a *zapusk* and, on the advice of the *promyshlenniki,* by killing off wifeless bulls, which, when rookeries were depleted, attracted the attention of hunters so obtuse they did not realize that their own persistent destruction of seal mothers was the cause of the herd's decline. To protect the little ones from being trampled when lonely males battled too fiercely for their share of the few cows, they contended that the unmated bulls must be destroyed, even though their scarred pelts were useless. In this wise, ignorant hunters set afoot the curious myth of the murderous males, which re-emerges from time to time to plague the fur seals.

The ill-kept records do not mention by name the intelligent Russian savior who recognized the necessity for preserving the *matki,* the mothers. By 1848, however, the experiment of exempting cows from death had been tried and adopted as a permanent policy; its effects so obviously beneficial that the injunction against killing females was rigidly enforced as long as the Russians remained in Alaska.

Other disasters befell the fur seals. The northern ice one winter—some say in 1835, blockaded St. Paul. Huddling in their unheated *ulux,* their seal oil and flesh exhausted, half the Aleut sealers died from hunger and cold. Far into the summer ice ringed the island and barred landing seals. Parturient mothers, unable to climb the steep barrier, drowned, convulsed by birth pains in the unnatural element of the sea.

A few social reforms were written into the second charter, more into the third. Colonial subjects were assigned to their social level; their rights and responsibilities defined. The Creoles, first generation offspring of marriages between a Russian and any native Alaskan, were made commoners, members of a very low middle class, tax-exempt, and eligible for Company employment. Meritorious conduct could advance them to a higher social rating. Ten years' colonial service was the price of an education in Russia and subsequent professional independence. The Aleuts and Kodiak Islanders, assigned to a special category as Russian subjects so long as they remained colonial residents, could, too, by outstanding achievements, climb higher socially—on paper at least. Tax-exempt as individuals, every community owed the Company the labor of half the male population between the ages of eighteen and fifty, but managers were obliged—again on paper—to outfit hunters and pay them no less than a fifth of the average Russian hunter's pay. Commandeering the services of all able-bodied individuals, male and female, colonial agents conducted affairs as usual, unimpressed by rules the Russian aristocratic directors must have considered most generous and most Christian, and shipped the Aleuts wherever they desired. When, in 1853, newly acquired Sakhalin Island was explored for fur-bearing animals, the Aleuts were ordered—not asked to volunteer—to provide twelve skin boats designed for two or three hunters, and to take their wives along to repair the boats and look after the hunters.

Shipping fur seal pelts to London in 1843 proved profitable. The next year sealskins and walrus ivory were sent to England and sealskins to New York, where they sold for high prices. New York furriers, practiced in handling pelts American ships brought back from the Southern Hemisphere, found plenty of buyers for seal coats for both sexes, seal caps, and carriage robes. Practical Yankees found that the heavy, warm sealskins never wore out. That the garments were bulky did not detract from their appeal. For quite a while seal furs were shipped almost every year to New York, occasionally other furs.

During the third charter the Company exported less than 400,000 sealskins and few sea otter furs. Annually Aleut hunters were supposed to receive goods worth 86 rubles as well as extra supplies for renting their boats. The Crown's stern injunction to the General Administration and its colonial agents to keep accurate financial records was never obeyed—the gap between policy and actual practices was too vast to reveal.

English and American trade at Canton gradually wiped out Russia's Chinese commerce. In 1862 duty-free tea crossed the Russian border. Kiakta trade came to a standstill. In desperation, the Russians packed seal and otter pelts by caravan to Peking. The skins were of poor quality; the journey long, dangerous, and unprofitable. Chinese merchants at border stations opened by special treaty in 1851 had no interest in furs. Frightened by dwindling dividends, the Company appealed to the Crown to permit the import of beaver and sealskins, with a high duty on the latter particularly, and to allocate a quarter of the tariff income to subsidize its Alaskan enterprise. To economize, in 1858 the Company began making seal oil for its ships and machinery. A thousand gallons from the Pribilofs that year saved them five thousand rubles—an economy achieved by the rash slaughter of many young seals; their small pelts were good for nothing except colonial clothing.

Despite lower profits, the Company sought to renew its charter in 1861. In a special, very critical report on colonial conditions, Captain Golovin supported its request. There was in St. Petersburg at the time a Creole of Aleut descent, the accomplished navigator Kashevarov, who had charted the Alaskan coast for the Company. He challenged Golovin's recommendation and denounced the Company's dreadful exploitation and humiliation of the Aleuts. Baron Wrangel, called on to refute Kashevarov's statements, admitted they were true. The Czar sent Prince Maksutov to Sitka to govern temporarily but let the Company, stripped of many powers and unprotected by a contract, continue its fur trade. A domestic incentive to maintain the colony vanished when the Russians no longer had to find exchange goods to satisfy Chinese market demands in order to obtain tea. The dry-souled profit seekers' indifference to all Alaska's products except furs had prevented colonization, expansion, and utilization of other resources. The pelt lovers of Irkutsk, whom Baranov had cursed, let treasures they did not dream existed slip from their greedy fingers because they failed to follow blueprints drawn by Shelekov, Baranov, and Rezanov. They stifled and finally stilled Baranov's Rioting Alaska. Their good fortune was based on the exploitation of the fur seals and the fur sealers. A single articulate Aleut exposed and over-threw them.

In another part of the world, men were dreaming of fur seal islands, banks of lava rocks where furs lay soft and gray and silky. So, in Washington, between midnight and dawn of a March night in 1867, in the presence of Ambassador Stoeckl, Mr. Seward signed his name to a document, and, for $7,200,-000, the fur seals and most of the sealers of the North Pacific became Americans.

The acquisition of the Alaskan seal islands was not the first American sealing venture. Long before 1867 American seamen had joined the hunting pack which overwhelmed the bear-headed seal of the South.

9

Wraiths of Austral Fur Seals

The Antarctic fur seal was never an empire builder, never the cornerstone of colonial enterprise; it was merely a drab counter in commercial transactions. A branch of the family of *Arctocephalus australis,* the bear-headed seal, contributed to the degeneration and extermination of the primitive inhabitants of Tierra del Fuego, but the southern sea bear's chief historic service was to shape the destinies of individual men, not to affect the march of nations. The austral fur seals elevated a few traders in Europe, New England, and China to the state of merchant princes, but they impoverished more men than they enriched. And their fatal, heavy, velvet fur brought misery or disaster, even death, to many of the hunters.

The massacre of the Antarctic fur seals began a few years before Pribylov discovered the last northern fur seal islands. The exact date of the inception of commercial sealing for furs in the Southern Hemisphere will never be known. Unchronicled seal slayers were operating before Captain Cook, after his discovery of South Georgia in 1775, called the beautiful silky-haired Georgian fur seals to the attention of commerce and advertised not only the location of that remote seal colony but also the one ready Pacific market for seal hides, the port of Canton, China. When the ship carrying Great Britain's special ambassador to China, Lord Macartney, anchored off New Amsterdam Island in the southern Indian Ocean in February 1773,

65

English and French seamen were busily killing 100 fur seals a day to fill an order for 25,000 sealskins for the Canton market.

As far as the written records reveal, the first Americans ventured into the seal fur trade somewhere in the Falkland Islands. In 1784 the *States* from Boston picked up 13,000 sealskins there and sold them in Boston for 50 cents each. Subsequently the same skins arrived in Calcutta, where their unscrupulous owner disposed of them, tagged "otter pelts," at $2 apiece. From India they went on to Canton to fetch—as sealskins—$5 each. Thereafter, without deceit or apology, southern sealskins taken by Americans went directly to Chinese markets—all but the few thousand skins American furriers could handle.

Within a decade, Canton-bound sealing ships—brigs, schooners, corvettes—were stopping off at the seal islands in the southern seas to get furs to exchange for spices, silk, nankeen, chinaware, and tea. The majority of the vessels were English and American, the latter sailing chiefly from the Connecticut and Long Island ports of New London, Stonington, Mystic, and Sag Harbor. The captains and crews of these vessels, famed as the "under-water fellows," generally combined sealing with whaling, elephant-seal oiling, or other trade. But during the thirty-five most profitable sealing years, from about 1790 to 1825, hundreds of vessels sailed from their home ports empty save for meager supplies and seal hunting equipment. They secured their trade goods—sealskins—and food rations—seal meat and seal oil—for the longest part of their run from the seal islands to Canton to sell the furs for cash or barter them for Chinese products. Though the Yankees and the British monopolized fur hunting in the Southern Hemisphere, all maritime nations had ships engaged in the trade; even the Russians finally investigated South Pacific sealing, but too late to offset their losses in the North.

It is difficult, from the incomplete records, to piece together a clear picture of the development of this kind of sealing. There is extant a letter written in 1791 by the captain of the *Britannia,* reputed also to be the first English whaler in those waters, noti-

fying the ship owners of his intention to run down to Amsterdam for a try at sealing. A year earlier Tristan da Cunha and
possibly nearby Gough Island in the Atlantic—from the latter
Captain Patten of Philadelphia took six thousand skins either
that year or the next—were sealed. The same year—perhaps
a little earlier—sealing for furs commenced along the west
African coast as far north as 20° south latitude. The skins from
this locality were undoubtedly the "gray beavers" the Czar
barred from his realm in 1802.

By 1792 several vessels were at the Falklands; at least one
of them on its maiden voyage with a green crew who had never
seen a fur seal. The same year, at Más Afuera in the Pacific,
Captain William Steward, of New York, obtained 38,000 sealskins which he sold at Canton for $16,000. These transactions
were secrets jealously guarded by most merchants, ship officers,
and crews; but, despite precaution, rumors drifted from port to
port, and more shipowners began to outfit ships. The discovery
of this unique horde of ready coinage lining the seaways to
China, free for the taking, excited the imagination and cupidity
of traders and seamen. Since to club a fur seal over the head
required no special skill, shipowners hired men useful afloat and
ashore. Such sailor-hunters received a "lay"—generally one per
cent of the profits—instead of regular wages; as usual only the
owners, and occasionally the captain, garnered the actual
profits.

Even while the Chinese used only tanned seal hides, they
would barter for the pelts, at a good rate of exchange, merchandise eagerly desired by America and Europe. But that was not
the only cause of the merchants' elation or the sole source of
their profits. The economies of a sealing voyage were many.
While killing seals, a crew could, on most seal islands, live on
local resources. The meat of marine mammals, seafowl and
their eggs, fresh fish and crustaceans were all tastier than salt
beef and other dried ship's rations. For the remainder of their
voyage the sealers could load their ships with food, fresh water,
oil for the ships' lights and grease, and, sometimes, firewood.

Handed on from one sealing vessel to another was an ingenious recipe for preserving bird eggs in sand and seal oil for the Pacific passage. Meaner economies were practiced by shipowners. Although their crews went sealing in the months of the southern summer, they were beset with wind, rain, and snowstorms. They bucked dangerous currents, encountered hidden reefs, and found few safe harbors. Yet owners failed to provide either trustworthy charts or navigating instruments. Some paid for their stingy preparations when their ships failed to return. But too many ships survived peril for the majority of owners to be frightened into the expenses of wise precautions.

Unlike the single-minded *promyshlenniki,* who were solely fur hunters, the southern sealers were seamen first and, only for intervals in midvoyage, hunters and seal slayers. Near most seal islands there were no primitive people like the Aleuts to enslave as hunters. Only as sealing waned did the small catches and low market price induce skippers to hire Maori hunters to go sealing near Australia for absurdly low wages.

At the beginning of southern sealing, when the beaches of countless islands were covered with fur, a vessel anchored offshore or cruised nearby while the crew quickly secured a full cargo of skins. As more vessels joined the chase and the fur seal herds dwindled, the custom of distributing small hunting gangs on several islands prevailed. Sealers, contemplating a year's residence or longer on an island, frequently erected huts, planted vegetable gardens, kept pigs, sheep, goats, and poultry to vary the monotonous local diet. While island provender was tastier than salt beef, it soon grew tiresome. For fish, shellfish, seals—hair and fur—and sea lions—even the birds—all smacked of fish. The meat of pigs and other domestic animals fattened on a seaweed or fish diet also acquired a fishlike flavor. Not all islands afforded sealers such luxuries. As protection against the inclement weather, too many hunters had only flimsy huts made of spars and canvas and subsisted on a seal diet.

When their vessel faded over the horizon, sealers had no

surety of her return on a promised date. She might be wrecked, captured by pirates at Macao, or suffer other accident. A sealing party on St. Felix expected relief at the end of three months, but it was many months later that another sailing vessel rescued them. In a South American port they learned the reason for their abandonment. Their captain had not been drowned at sea; he had been long submerged in liquor in the dives of the Peruvian port of Callao. Sobering from his spree, he found himself penniless, his ship seized to pay his debts, and all means of rescuing his men and his furs gone.

As sealing vessels sought their quarry nearer the Antarctic Circle, they faced the menace of icebergs, the hazard of being caught and crushed in the ice fields. Not exaggerated are the vicissitudes of the two sealing ships which James Fenimore Cooper, himself an owner of sealing vessels, dramatized in his novel *The Sea Lions*.

If hunting fur seals were not dangerous, the voyages to and from their islands were extremely hazardous. Worse than the poverty which rewarded the toil and endurance of most sealers —earning with haphazard success a single per cent of the net profits—was the sea's wrath. Moll Pitcher, aged seeress of Lynn, frightened off the first two crews signed on the newly built *Massachusetts,* with her prophecy that the vessel would perish on her maiden trip. Moll was mistaken. The *Massachusetts,* manned by her third crew, about 60 officers and men, weathered her first run to Canton via the seal islands; but, within less than 20 years, about 50 of that company were dead, most of them having died at sea or far from home a year or two after that first Canton trip. For the sailor who fell from the mainyard, there was a grave in Batavia. Five perished at Macao, four murdered by river pirates, one rotted by leprosy. Storms swept two overboard in Japanese waters; three succumbed at the River Plate, and one off Cape Horn. Two were lost on separate return trips to Canton, another heading toward Bombay, still another aboard a British Indiaman, and one more in the Straits of Sunda. Two with the Northwest Coast Survey were buried at sea; another died ashore—in England, not at home. Whampoa, outpost of Canton, was the last port of call for six: one drowned, one dead of smallpox, one murdered and the others of unreported causes. Twenty others had died here and there in the oceans of the world or in alien ports. And one, most unfortunate of all, lived—a prisoner in Algiers.

The sea taxed all sailing vessels; there were no exemptions for sealers. If she demanded no toll one trip, she asked for compound interest on another. Singularly fortunate was the sealing ship that skirted the stormy regions of *Arctocephalus* and came back round the world to its port without having left a man or two somewhere along the way to satisfy the sea's insatiable hunger for tribute. Yet there were always volunteers to go sealing, expecting gain from their small share of the take—too many, in fact, so that furs grew scarce and ships faced into new waters to find more seal islands. The hunt for furs intensified and the slaughter of 1800, the year after the Russian monopoly was organized in the north, was the most bloodily destructive. Thirty American ships and many more from other lands scattered sealing gangs over the known islands and some newly discovered. On the islands neighboring New Zealand every living seal was attacked. Eighteen bands of hunters, the first party killing 57,000 fur seals before competitors arrived, almost depopulated the South Georgian rookeries. The tardier hunters divided among themselves another 65,000 furs. The Sandwich and Bouvet Islands became regular sealing stations after that season.

Erroneously charted by their discoverer—more truly only a passing observer—the Crozet Islands had been vainly sought by sealers for so many seasons that they had begun to seem a mirage, a shadow on the horizon or a floating ice mass that Crozet had mistaken for solid land. Sailing back and forth in the neighborhood of the purported latitudes in 1805, Captain Henry Fanning located the five islands: Pig, East, Possession, Penguin, and the Seven Apostles. Putting hunters ashore, he returned to Prince Edward Island—its beaches were being sealed for the first time that year—to leave sailing instructions for another of his firm's ships to pick up the Crozet gang and their furs. The Prince Edward sealers watched suspiciously as he buried a message under a heap of rocks, the usual communication system of whalers and sealers. Succumbing to the envious hope they might learn of new fur seal resorts, they opened the cache as soon as Fanning left. From the buried papers they learned nothing. The real information had been secretly hidden at another spot, cannily arranged for before sailing. Meanwhile Fanning's men on the Crozet beaches were disturbed by the arrival of two other vessels. Cruising in search of the elusive islands, both ships had succeeded in imitating Fanning's good fortune. Since fur seals were plentiful, the three gangs hunted without quarreling over a division of territory or spoils. The boat, directed there by Fanning, found a large catch of salted skins waiting to be loaded aboard.

So ruthlessly thorough was the killing on all the rookeries of the southern sea bear that by 1811 the regular seal coinage banks had failed. More and more frequently, American ships made mixed voyages, picking up a few furs here and there, chasing a whale, boiling down the huge elephant seals and other fatty creatures. On the way back to New England the oil was frequently traded in Brazil for coffee. Flooded with pelts of the northern fur seal, so much finer in quality than the skins of many species of the southern genus, China was no longer a profitable market. Yet the sealers were discouraged neither by low price nor the lack of seals. Always over the horizon, they believed, lay undiscovered beaches to which the fur seals had fled. Larger cargoes of furs would make up for the lower prices. Consequently, many vessels sailed to seek hidden seal haunts in the loneliest and coldest waters of the south. Macquarie Island was found. Within a year its discoverer had killed 80,000 fur seals there. Eight years later the thick-furred seals of the New Shetland group were located. During the first year, 30 vessels—18 American, 10 English, and 2 Russian—plundered the rich treasure. At least 600,000 Shetland sealskins went to

market before 1822. More than 100,000 orphaned pups starved
on their birthrocks, and innumerable thousands of fetuses were
destroyed unborn. After just two seasons of killing, the fur
hunters knew it was futile to stop off at the Shetlands for pelts.

Sporadically, during the rest of the 19th century, seal hunting
continued in the Southern Hemisphere. Each time survivors of
earlier massacres succeeded in recreating large colonies, news
of their renascence would reach the ears of hunters. Within a
few years those beaches would be desolated again.

After 1870, for instance, when the sealers went south again,
they found that many herds in the loneliest, coldest high-south
latitudes had recuperated. It was a recrudescence soon snuffed
out. On the remotest beaches the reinvigorated herds were
killed off down to the last baby seal. From South Georgia there
came a rumor of an illegal catch in 1907. The New England
prowler got off safely with his haul. Years later, in 1915, a Nor-
wegian sailor met one—one lonely furred waif—on a beach
there. Implacably he executed the solitary representative—perhaps the very last—of the wondrous furred Georgian beauties
exposed to man's greed by Captain Cook.

From most of their islands there have come no recent tidings
of living descendants of the bear-headed seals. Fugitives there
may be in lonely byways, gliding like shadows through isolated
interisland channels and quiet bays (waters which their ancestors filled with busy, pulsating crowds), hauling out forlornly
on their worn, deserted ancestral rocks, to breed, perhaps. Perhaps only to die.

The first hunting had been the fierce swoop of vulturous killers on their defenseless beaches. The second had resembled a
flock of birds scuttling about a fresh-reaped field to pick up
stray seeds the harvesters left behind. The scant pickings the
hunters bore to the London market were gainful. For, far from
the seal islands, along the avenues of the world's great cities,
the fashionable ladies strolled in their fur seal sacques. Sealskins were the mode. So, prying and snooping diligently, the
relentless hunters prowled among the seal rocks, harrying the

last pitiful fugitive from hiding. The killers were patient and painstaking in their searchings. When they retired, manifold seal islands were empty. No third rapacious, wide-ranging, hemispheric pursuit of the bear-headed seal can ever come to pass. The course of most species of the austral seal had closed by 1890—roughly a century after that obscure Chinese inventor's genius transmuted sealskin into seal fur and convoked the hunting pack.

Until Alaskan seal furs became fashionable, no nation had taken steps to protect its fur seals in the Southern Hemisphere except Uruguay. In 1876 the government of Uruguay, spurred by a denunciatory campaign waged by politically hostile newspapers, revised its earlier leasing system. The reforms were inadequate. The lessees were forbidden to kill seals between October and June. But throughout the remainder of the year they could kill as many seals as they desired, including females and young ones. Before the end of the century several hundred thousand Lobos Island skins taken under this system had been exported to London. But in 1910 the American agent of Lampson and Sons—that firm did not handle Lobos pelts—noted that a competitor's sales catalogue contained no advertisement of pelts from Uruguay. The export has remained irregular until very recently. The failure to save the seal mothers had its usual baleful and inevitable consequence.

The news of the regular annual sale of a hundred thousand Alaskan seals and the United States' new income from sealskin duty inspired other nations after 1870 to seek a regular income from their depleted herds. Feeble regulations were instituted by Argentina, Chile, Mexico, and governors and parliaments of districts of the British Empire. Motivated chiefly by a desire to secure national revenue, none of these measures were genuine conservation programs. Licensing killers saved no seal lives. Establishing closed seasons and penalties for poachers were rudimentary restrictions, in most instances ineffectual except to collect fines imposed too late to save the seals from death. Whether or not at an earlier date their herds would have been worth the expense of armed patrols was already an academic question when lawmakers realized the rich natural resource their countries had lost.

The belated measures to defend the seals on the few outposts that remained have saved a few thousand animals. Some South African skins come to market, over 29,000 of them in 1957, but these pelts are not of a high quality. In the same year nearly 5,500 undressed skins from Uruguay's Lobos Islands were exported to the United States, the only world market for raw seal pelts. Chile and Mexico try to protect the small number left on their islands. Australia watches over scattered seal colonies, determined they shall enjoy the peace they require to increase and multiply. Seals began to visit her Macquarie Island, for instance, about thirty years ago but none bred there until about 1955. Already the clan of *Arctocephalus fosteri* numbers several hundred members. There is now ground for hope that the Antarctic fur seal will escape extinction and may even become a commercial resource in some baker's dozen of islands. But the beaches of the Southern Hemisphere which will never harbor breeding fur seals again are legion. There exists but little reason to hope that *Arctocephalus* will ever catch up with, much less surpass in numbers, his more fortunate relatives of the North Pacific.

10

The Northern Fur Seal
Becomes an American

A furred wraith flitted wordlessly between the lines of the formal documents of the Alaska Transfer; took shape as one item among the many resources catalogued in Senator Sumner's defense of Seward's privy acquisition of Walrussia. Twenty-five years later, before an international tribunal called to decide the fur seals' nationality, American statesmen publicly confessed that they and their islands had been the sole golden incentive to purchase "Seward's Ice Box." Then, the lack of letters and printed texts to uphold the fur seals' right to American citizenship damaged the plaintiff's suit. In 1867 the fur seal was not a public figure.

The obscurity was deliberate. The one resource Americans had learned most about during Russia's occupation of Alaska had been the fur seal. Exchanging their goods for its pelts and visiting the Seal Islands to collect their pay, Yankee traders had been most observant. The legislature of the Territory of Washington memorialized Congress in 1866 to buy Alaska for its fisheries. If no one in the city of Washington had heard of seal fisheries, residents of the Capital's territorial namesake had. Secretly, California merchants urged Seward to lease or buy the Russian fur empire—for them as their own private property, it was reported. Their eloquence induced the Secretary of State to buy it for the whole nation. Pressure from citizens of the West Coast was admitted after the purchase. One purpose had locked the lips of the informed: the ambition to be first at the kill on the Seal Islands.

On October 18, 1867, guns booming through the foggy dusk of an autumn afternoon in Sitka saluted the Stars and Stripes as it rose to proclaim American Alaska. No echo rolled north to the islands in the Bering where the fur seals, unaware that their future was being planned in Sitka, were winding up their seasonal affairs. A farsighted Baltimore merchant, Hayward Hutchinson, anxious to invest the fortune he had made selling shoes during the Civil War, had come to Sitka as a member of the American official party, ostensibly as secretary to General Rousseau. Issued a special landing permit, he went ashore early in the morning and spent the day bargaining with Prince Maksutov, acting agent for the Russian-American Company, from whom he bought, for the trifling sum of $155,000, the ships and the entire stock of merchandise, buildings, and equipment of the retiring Russian firm, including its property on the Pribilofs and the Commander Islands. He hired its former Creole and Russian employees for salaries higher than their previous wages. The same intent to monopolize the fur trade of the North Pacific, especially its stable nucleus, the fur seals, had led a dozen or more West Coast merchants to Sitka, but Hutchinson's special shore pass and early rising frustrated them.

During the winter the firm of Hutchinson, Kohl and Company was organized. Kohl was a British Columbia merchant. Gustave Niebaum, former officer of the Russian company, secured a partnership due to his rather inexplicable personal possession of a cargo of seal pelts. Hutchinson's Midas touch did not fail during the organization of the new firm. He transferred to the company for $10,000, a Russian ship which had cost him only $4,000. Part of the tea, metal, and dry goods he sold in San Francisco for $100,000 more than he had paid for all Russian equipment.

Other merchants, too, spent that winter outfitting ships and crews to go hunting Pribilof fur seals. In the spring several vessels arrived at St. George, stocked with food and clothing to trade the Aleuts for sealskins. There had been rumors of the impending transfer, but the appearance of American traders was confirmation that the fur seals and their Aleut sealers had a new nationality and new masters. The newcomers, nominally recognizing the Aleuts as the real owners of the furred animals of their home islands, a viewpoint soon obliterated by events and a Congressional decree that their home islands were animal reservations, ironically investing the land title in the seals and not the sealers, offered to buy sealskins for thirty cents apiece and pay in goods—and liquor. One vessel brought only liquor— cleared at Customs to sell in Siberia. The chief investor in that transaction, too pious to buy furs of animals slaughtered on the Sabbath, profited from weekday liquor sales to debauch people.

The first landing party on St. George was a crew sent by the San Francisco firm of Parrot and Company. Led by Agent Howe, they took possession of the salthouses. Hutchinson, Kohl and Company representatives, armed with proof of ownership of buildings and tools, landed a few days later. Then Captain Morgan, an experienced South Sea sealer, arrived with assistants to acquire skins for the New London traders, Williams and Haven. Hutchinson had henchmen more useful than a veteran sealer. His chief aide, the old Creole navigator Captain Archimandritov, who had visited the Pribilofs in 1864 as the Russians' colonial inspector, commanded the prompt obedience of the non-English speaking inhabitants. Dr. Dall of the Smithsonian Institution, collecting St. George sea shells that summer, reported sealers trembled with terror in his presence. The captain announced that his American employer was the sole legal successor to the Russians—less lie than prophecy. Demanding obedience in the name of a higher authority than Hutchinson or the Czar, an Orthodox Russian priest threatened the islanders with eternal punishment if they did not render unto Hutchinson all that he asked. Advised by the priest and Captain Archimandritov, the Aleuts obediently accepted a five-year contract to kill seals for Hutchinson's agents.

Wisely yielding to superior advantages, the two unpropertied agents agreed to accept a quarter each of the season's catch while Hutchinson's men retained half. As partners averse to more competition, they drove off all others who tried to land sealing crews, among them the Russian vice-consul at Honolulu, Mr. Pfluger. Confident Americans were ignorant of Pribilof resources, he was disagreeably amazed to find the islands occupied. On St. Paul, a similar compromise was arranged between the three earliest competitors, with the major benefits accruing to Hutchinson, Kohl and Company, legal owners of the salthouses.

On both islands, except for the wanton taking of human life, it appeared that the *promyshlenniki* had come again. No matter what language fur hunters spoke, their behavior was unbridled and licentious. While male Aleuts killed seals, and skinned and salted their pelts, the Americans camped out in the semiunderground dwellings of their hosts, drinking and making love to island women.

During that frightful summer of slaughter, the Aleut seal guardians stoutly refused to kill cows. Old sealers had witnessed in their lifetime the rebirth and maintenance of a flourishing herd as soon as the lives of mother seals were spared. No consideration for male life, however, stayed their clubs. Others besides Dr. Dall suspected that many skins were shipped to foreign ports, particularly to the Sandwich or Hawaiian Islands. The summer's death total was probably higher than 365,000, Agent Howe's estimate and a figure rivaling early Russian excesses. Only the sealers' physical fatigue determined the daily toll. On St. Paul, according to the whaler Captain Daniel Webster, sealing ended while killable seals were still numerous, only because the salt supply was exhausted.

Rumors of reckless slaying filtered through to Washington where, on July 27, 1868, Congress prohibited further destruction of seal life until a legal method of handling the industry had been devised. Notice of the restriction reached the Pribilofs that autumn, about the time Hutchinson and his friends arrived in Washington to persuade Congress to lease sealing rights to one firm—his company, of course, as an established Pribilof property owner—for 99 years. The compromise reached by the agents of rival companies during the sealing of 1868 was perpetuated by their joining forces to organize the Alaska Commercial Company in time to bid for the first franchise in 1870— a lease which a cautious Congress, despite the group's influence and 2-year campaign of threats and arguments, limited to a 20-year period. Even so, Hutchinson and his partners could be proud of their lobbying efforts. They had bested diligent rivals who also possessed powerful political friends, including members of Congress.

While the political air in Washington seethed with the pros and cons of sealing rights, Captain Henriques, of the revenue steamer *Lincoln,* belatedly introduced American law to St. Paul in May 1869. He landed a company of soldiers, headed by a revenue Marine lieutenant, and a special Treasury agent, Dr. H. H. McIntyre. Two months previously another special agent had reached St. Paul—the retired whaler Captain Charles Bryant, who had been farming in Massachusetts for a decade prior to 1868. Captain Henriques ordered the assembled St. Paul sealers to kill their dogs and surrender their guns to Lieutenant Barnes for the duration of the seals' stay. The survivors of the previous summer's massacre were to be spared visits of wandering dogs and the sound of gunfire. The Russians, convinced that seals undisturbed by hunters would not be frightened by ordinary noises, had never exercised similar precautions. No sealer objected. Within ten minutes all dogs on the island had been executed; all guns surrendered. The instant unprotesting compliance, which astounded Henriques, suggests that a summer of American occupation had convinced the sealers that the newcomers were no more lenient taskmasters than their former Russian overseers. Barnes gave the Aleuts permission to kill thirty thousand seals for food. More were taken, the Treasury was informed by Special Agent Wiker, who arrived later in the season. His personal investigation was obstructed by local officials who showed him only skins stored in three salthouses. Accidentally, he stumbled on an outlying shed stacked with more pelts. Friendly Aleuts confided that many skins had already been shipped on whaling vessels before his arrival, probably bound for Honolulu or another convenient foreign harbor. Returning to the States in the autumn, Dr. McIntyre requested that the soldiers be withdrawn. Their conduct undermined Pribilof morals. Cynics sneered that, free to prowl about the islands, soldiers had proved inconvenient snoopers, able to tell too much about actual local happenings. They were transferred.

Convinced that information they had collected as Government servants had influenced the Treasury Department and Congress, McIntyre counted the decision to lease sealing rights to a single private firm a triumph for Bryant and himself. How much his hope of lucrative employment in private industry swayed his judgment could have been accurately appraised only by his own conscience. Because, as soon as Congressional consent was assured, McIntyre forsook his minor Treasury post to become, in June 1870, the general agent of the Alaska Commercial Company and, in August, their Superintendent of Seal Fisheries, a position he filled until 1889. At the time of the Transfer, the experienced Russians considered 76,000 a maximum yearly catch, so, especially after the heavy killing of 1868, McIntyre's recommendation of an annual quota of 100,000 seals seems peculiarly generous. He was the forerunner of too many Government sealing officials to be suspected of more devotion to Hutchinson than to the interests of fur seals or the American public.

Hutchinson's efforts to round up legislative support in Washington for the leasing system, begrudgingly seconded by competitors seeking the lease for themselves, met some opposition. Secretary of the Treasury Boutwell's mistrust of a Pribilof

Henry Wood Elliott

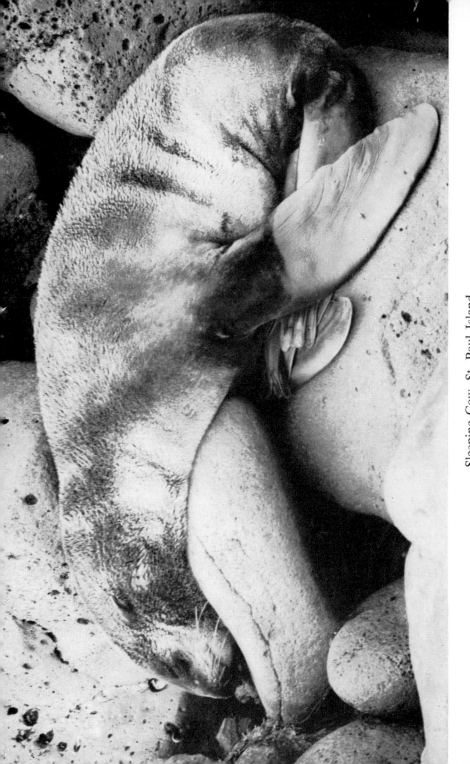

Sleeping Cow, St. Paul Island

monopoly was vigorously backed up by many, including Special Agent Wiker and William Sumner Dodge, first American Mayor of Sitka. Their radical proposals shocked conventional business minds: sealing confined to the experienced Aleuts under Government supervision; public auction of salted skins under the same auspices; a tax on each skin to augment national income; and, after the industrial expenses of management and auctioneering were deducted from the gross sales, liberal compensation to sealers—not merely as wages, but in recognition of their inherent rights in the animals. Faint reverberations of the ideals that had just successfully freed the slaves inspired the plea for Aleut participation in sealing proceeds, echoes weak and thin, soon silenced by the brassy chorus of commercial interests.

Uncertain whether or not a monopoly was consonant with American philosophy, Dr. Dall warned that if the fur seals were to survive private industry's management, Government agents must receive salaries high enough to counteract offers of bribery. Because he considered even the Creoles, despite their superior advantages, too dirty and lazy to be American citizens, Treaty or no Treaty, Dall did not support claims for Aleut ownership. The Aleuts asked only that Captain Ilarion Archimandritov be recognized as their representative. Archimandritov, Hutchinson's man, an individual from whom, as Dr. Dall testified, the sealers recoiled in terror when he walked near them, was hardly their voluntarily selected spokesman. But the captain had a talent for soliciting Aleut signatures. Hutchinson had built up impregnable defenses.

Congress authorized the leasing of the Seal Islands in July 1870. The Treasury immediately advertised for bids. Three were submitted by the Alaska Commercial Company, two definite rent proposals and an offer to pay more than any other bidder. Six years later the public learned how valuable Hutchinson's Sitka shopping expedition had been, that it had won his firm the right to kill 100,000 young male seals each summer for 20 years in exchange for an annual rent of $55,000 and a tax on each skin of $2.62½. The tax was almost as high as the current selling price, but, since furriers and their customers were beginning to display more interest in sealskins, prices had begun to rise. His Company was to supply the sealers each year, without charge, 25,000 dried salmon, 60 cords of firewood, and barrels sufficient to store their winter supply of seal meat, and provide a physician and a teacher for each island. The Company could charge 25 per cent more for goods it sold the sealers in its store than retail San Francisco prices—a privilege practically impossible for a Treasury agent to supervise. Harking back to that wonderful summer of 1868, when competition kept the prices reasonable, the sealers grumbled over high prices for years. Several times before they finally grasped the economic principle of monopoly and accepted their lot, they boldly petitioned that other stores be permitted on their islands. For each slaughtered seal, the Company paid 40 cents into a communal wage fund from which each worker received a "share" in accordance with his rating as a skilled sealer. A first-class share in 1872 was $421.22; a fourth-class, $315.85.

Hutchinson's ruthlessness and shrewdness won him the monopoly of the Alaskan fur seal. And the fur seal enabled his Company to obstruct Alaska's development. In vain the Territory's governors protested that the Company, fearful lest newcomers would interfere with their fur trade, supported paid lobbyists in Washington to block all legislation to promote investment and colonization. While they pleaded futilely with national Government officers to rescind Hutchinson's franchise and free Alaska from the chains of the fur seals' master, that gentleman was busy on the other side of the North Pacific, acquiring control of the remaining northern fur seals.

On February 18, 1871 Hutchinson, Kohl, Maksutov and Company was awarded a twenty-year contract to seal on the Commander and Robben Islands. The contract was kept secret until, in the early summer, Hutchinson's representatives landed on the Commander Islands and dispossessed the unauthorized incumbent, the Ice Company of San Francisco—an odd name for a fur-collecting company. Warned off from the Pribilofs in 1868, Pfluger had secured Commander furs without interference. How many traders had the same success is not known, but, for three summers, many had brought goods and alcohol to the Aleuts, occasioning worse slaughter and debauchery than the Pribilofs knew in 1868. Drinking parties on the rookeries numbed sealer consciences. Intoxicated Aleuts stumbled blindly among the rocks, massacring without discrimination, slaughtering thousands of females. The estimate that 65,000 skins were taken was but a random and ridiculously moderate guess. After three successive summers of such insane killing, Hutchinson's men found the rookeries almost bare. Transferring Captain Daniel Webster from the Pribilofs to maintain order and improve sealing methods, several years passed before the Americans could kill enough seals to make the lease profitable.

Soon Maksutov's name disappeared. To comply with the law that at least one citizen be a member of any firm conducting business inside Russia, the Company paid a Siberian merchant, Mr. Phillipeus, for the use of his name. Nominally, Hutchinson, Kohl, Phillipeus and Company was Russian; its American ships flew the Russian flag. Later interlocking between Hutchinson's two interests occurred, and, until 1893, when the Czar's refusal to renew the lease was announced, all transactions of the alleged Russian company were directed from 310 Sansome Street, San Francisco, U.S.A., the Alaska Commercial Company's address. The office maintained in Petropavlovsk only guided the Company's furs through Russian custom formalities and purchased Siberian land furs. Hutchinson proved to be a better empire builder—for his own gain—than Shelekov.

Even he could err. Too late his agents learned of other northern fur seals. In 1875 the Czar traded the Kuril Islands to Japan for the southern half of Sakhalin Island. The small colony of Aleut hunters, removed from the Kurils to Kamchatka but finally settled with their own kin on the Commander Islands, brought news of Kuril rookeries. In 1881 Captain Sandeman, a Commander Island sealing officer, visited the Middle Kurils

and sailed around Srednoi Rocks, but saw no seals where, later
that year, more fortunate visitors, arriving after migrants had
returned from their sea travels, secured nearly eight thousand
pelts. As soon as English, American, and even Dutch, vessels
learned the way to the Kuril rookeries, the population shrank
so rapidly it was soon too small to tempt Hutchinson. He had
reached his goal. Save for those few thousand animals on the
Kuril rocks, the North Pacific fur seals had become American
property—and his.

11

A Pribilof Romance

In 1872, during the second year of Hutchinson's reign, a doomed young man entered the heart of the fur seal kingdom of St. Paul Island. Perched awkwardly astride a luggage-laden sled, drawn slowly across the snow from Lukannon's shore by Aleut sealers, he held his nose as the fetid odor of rotting seal assaulted his already squeamish, sea-weary senses. His "unmitigated sensations of disgust" overpowered any faint prescient whisper that he was about to enter the lists as a lifelong champion of a most grievously wronged animal. An assistant Treasury agent, he bore a verbal commission from the Smithsonian Institution to study the fur seal, still an enigma to American scientists. Before he recovered his land legs, he was hurried off to Northeast Point that afternoon to check the lessees' count of furs being loaded aboard the *Alexander*—a prosaic introduction to his vocation.

Amazed to find local government as well as commercial managers so indifferent to all aspects of seal life except collecting marketable furs that they had never tried to count the herd or explore the shore line of the islands, Henry Wood Elliott found himself elected by circumstances to be the fur seals' interpreter. A zealous and indefatigable unveiler of Pribilof mysteries, laden with notebook, sketch pad, and surveying instruments, he made his way against the Bering's fierce winds over the roughest boulder patches and through the heavy sand, taking measurements for his maps—the first—of the Seal Islands and jotting down his observations. Soon after his arrival, the first beachmasters hauled out. Day after day he haunted the seal beaches until dusk, even keeping night watches to see if any bull napped during the dark hours. Reading his rhapsodies, it is easy to picture him sprawled out on the rocks gazing fondly into fur seal eyes.

"Indeed, there are few eyes in the orbits of men and women which suggest more pleasantly the ancient thought of their being 'windows of the soul.' The lids to the eye are fringed with long, perfect lashes." This is Elliott's description of the protruding eyes of a young fur seal. He was as eloquent about its mother. "The large, lustrous blue-blackish eyes are humid and soft with the tenderest expressions." Of the adult male he wrote seriously: "The light framework of the skull supports an expressive pair of large bluish-hazel eyes; alternately burning with revengeful passionate light, then suddenly changing to the tones of tenderness and good nature." The voice of the lover is heard throughout Henry Wood Elliott's monograph on the fur seal.

Actually he had a pedantic nature. Meticulously detailed were his field notes. His drawing pencil less adroit, his fur seals have a wooden quality, stolid square proportions that distort their lissom, streamlined contours. Fifty years later an Aleut woman of St. George Island burned a copy of his monograph because she thought that his Aleut faces, "all alike, looking like boxes and very ugly," were an insult to her people. The fur seal was unable to protest the artistic affronts of its admirer.

Many dated sketches indicate Elliott was extremely busy in June and July. Yet he found time to court the handsome, educated eighteen-year-old Alexandra Melovidov and marry her in St. Paul's picturesque Russian church on July 12th. When Alaska became American, her Creole father, a former colonial official in Sitka, removed his family to St. Paul where Americans were astounded to meet the most perfect hostess of their acquaintance, Alexandra's mother, in such a remote, rude village. Even blessed with her mother's charm, Alexandra must have been extraordinarily attractive to divert Elliott from his fur seals during the delirium of discovery.

Undisturbed by doubts which caused another agent to exclaim, "It would be about as easy to calculate the number of bees in and around a hive," Elliott solved to his own satisfaction the complications of counting seals—at least the mating seals and their young. Convinced from his observations that rookery animals occupied any given rod of beach in exactly the same ratio of animals to area, he postulated a law "of uniform distribution" of breeders. During the mating season, an unknown natural inhibition, he asserted, prevented their crowding closer together or spreading out to cover more territory, no matter how much empty beach space was available. He calculated the mean space occupied by an average seal, an imaginary animal, to which he allowed two square feet of beach surface. It is rather difficult to understand how he fabricated this mythical seal from the disparate sizes of a bull, a cow, and a pup. Dividing the square footage of the rookery by two, he arrived at his census total. St. Paul's rookeries contained over 3 million seals in 1873; St. George's narrower beaches, only 160,000.

The mobility of nonbreeding classes defeated his mathematical powers. The number of frisky, peripatetic bachelors and restless yearlings could, he conceded, be conjectured only by a seasonal observer of the hauling grounds. He estimated that there were that summer another million and a half of these age groups, perhaps more. The teeming host of furred animal life that the beaches contained made his senses reel. No violence of man could ever destroy, even damage, such prolific fecundity.

The fur seal's adaptation to a double life on land and sea, which Elliott considered proof of the animal's "superiority from a purely physical point of view," actually branded it as a creature on the downgrade, reversing evolutionary ascent. Its instincts, which he praised for rivaling human intelligence, were really a rigid, unbreakable chain, keeping it irrevocably hobbled within reach of the sealer's club and knife. Elliott saw no blemishes. The fur seal was the most perfect of nature's creatures.

The fur seal kingdom had some defects. The sealers' drinking, usually with the encouragement or connivance of officials, disturbed him; but he expected his recommendations would lead to the abolition of all loose conduct. Since he deemed no circumstances could be more advantageous for man and animal than the administration of Mr. Hutchinson's Company, he foresaw a bright future for seals and sealers. Not that any lessee could subvert the fur seals' natural guardians. If the herd, which was the Pribilof Aleuts' sole livelihood, was abused, all 398 islanders could not be bribed or intimidated to keep silent. They would, at least, complain to Unalaskan relatives; the gossip would spread to the outside world.

The ill-paid post of Treasury agent, bestowed as a political reward, entailed two definite tasks: a count of salted skins that the lessees shipped and the supervision of store prices to prevent Company overcharging. New appointees had to rely on the experienced permanent Company staff to acquaint them with sealing matters, a reliance too easily become habitual, and for an agreeable social life—disagreement with Company personnel would make their island stay intolerably lonely and miserable. Fatally their tenure swung on the tide of presidential elections. Many names, signed to the annual reassurances to the Treasury of the flourishing conditions of Pribilof animal and human life, appeared, when a new President took office, on the lessees' payroll. A reliable employer, the Company never automatically discharged a faithful servant after four years' service. Aware of local conditions and the handicaps the agents faced, Elliott proposed only that they be transported on Government cutters to silence gossip that they accepted free passage on Company boats in return for ignoring infractions of its franchise. As long as lessees were as honorable as the Alaska Commercial Company, Elliott had no qualms about apathetic, corruptible agents.

Or about the Aleut sealers he once defined as members of a lower race, mere "passive killers of time," drinking tea and sleeping between sealing seasons. Then, he admitted, they

worked with astounding celerity and efficiency. During his first
summer 71 men killed and skinned 75,000 seals in 50 working
days. The next year the same gang secured that quota in 40
days; while 90,000 fur seals were skinned in only 39 days in
1874. They earned their annual salary in a few weeks. Except
for occasional odd jobs for the Company and fox trapping in
winter, there was no work for them between sealing seasons.
Gamblers were "disagreeable exceptions" to the indolent. Elliott deplored their addiction to games of chance which the
Russians and the Americans had taught them. To amuse themselves, the Americans gave the too quiet sealers strong spirits
to loosen their tongues and start them dancing. Only member-
ship in the Russian Orthodox Church preserved the sealers from
"utter stagnation." The Russian legacy of religion was the
nucleus of Aleut cultural and intellectual life. The Aleuts, Elliott
admitted, were as devoutly Christian as any churchgoers in the
States, yet he considered liquor suppliers and gambling instruc-
tors their racial superiors. The sealers interested him only because geographic and historic accidents had made them the
natural custodians of his fur seals.

The Treasury Department was warned that the Company
was building cheap, small frame houses in order to play the old
Sitka game when their lease expired—to claim renewal of its
franchise as owner of Pribilof buildings. Even Elliott realized
that enlightened business policy, not philanthropy, moved the
sealers from their native huts to civilized wooden houses. The
Aleuts, warmer, even less crowded, in their semiunderground,
sod-roofed huts, adapted to a windy climate on treeless islands
thousands of miles from coal mines, asked permission to erect
their own homes on ground reserved for their sole use. The
Company accused them of plotting to establish their right to
perpetual Pribilof residence and overruled their petition. Perhaps they were. (The Russians claimed title only to plots on
which their own buildings stood. Otherwise all land belonged
to its native inhabitants.) The time when a disillusioned Elliott
would fulminate against the enormous reparations the dispos-

sessed lessees claimed for those cottages was far off. Watching them going up, he was gratified at the introduction of American mores and ignored the Aleuts' inability to heat the flimsy dwellings. Until 1890, Elliott accepted the jerry-built houses and perfunctory educational and medical services as almost more than the Aleuts' due.

With Alexandra, a baby daughter, and his boxes of botanical specimens, which molded on the trip to San Francisco, Elliott returned to the States in the early autumn of 1873, an impatient comet streaking from the North to acquaint the world with the life story of the Pribilof fur seal. Acclaim was immediate. Soon he was referred to respectfully as Professor Elliott, the great fur seal authority, the sole expert on fur seal matters—dangerous homage to a young man not yet thirty and already intoxicated by the wonder of his discovery. Yet, if he seemed insufferably vain in later years, always announcing "I was the first," he was the first to bare the secrets of Pribilof fur seal life. Over a hundred years after Steller's discovery of the Commander sea bears, Elliott had found their Pribilof cousins.

To check his seal count, the Treasury sent Elliott back in 1874, accompanied by a young New England naval officer, Lieutenant (later Admiral) Washburn Maynard. The lieutenant brought more reliable surveying instruments and a more objective attitude toward the fur seals, but he judged Elliott's computation of nonbreeding seals too low. Three million bachelors and yearlings had visited the Pribilofs in 1873, Maynard decided, making the total seal population nearly six millions. Lieutenant Maynard recommended an obligatory annual rookery survey and a calculation of the total number of animals. Had his simple, wise precaution been observed, the fur seal herd would have escaped years of persecution, and American prestige would not have been soiled in international councils by indisputable proof of negligence.

In 1876 the pack of disappointed bidders, who had been baying for Hutchinson's overthrow, induced Congress to investigate his acquisition of the seal franchise and administration of the Seal Islands. Since visitors were excluded from the Pribilof animal reservation, there were no unbiased witnesses to testify. The accusers presented scant factual evidence to substantiate charges of bribery, corruption, killing above the quota, and exploitation of the sealers. Too patently tinged with anxiety to divert Pribilof profits into their own pockets, their testimony sounded unconvincing and was contradicted by reputable witnesses, many of them Government officers. Ex-Government employees who criticized the lessees had a record of clashing with Company personnel, and were easily discredited as embittered and vengeful. Hutchinson's flimsy frame houses were frequently mentioned as convincing exponents of the lessees' true character.

Against the pronouncements of the most important witness for the defense of the monopoly system, the renowned fur seal authority, Professor Elliott, cavils of jealous men could not prevail. Reasonably, the Congressional committee concluded the Alaska Commercial Company and its remarkable Mr. Hutchinson had been guilty of no more heinous offenses than foresight, bold action, and success.

Since the sealing monopoly was invulnerable, its opponents turned on its chief apologist whose armor had many chinks. The "natural foe" of Alaska, William Gouverneur Morris and others called him, a "penny-liner," cheaply prostituting his scientific and journalistic ability to strangle Alaskan progress. As a hireling of the Alaska Commercial Company, he was only too successful in reaching the uninformed public with his propaganda, mourned his defamers. If, as his enemies claimed, the Alaska Commercial Company paid him as a consultant on fur seal problems—he once admitted accepting a retainer but insisted he had never been employed by it or any other private firm for a salary—they had wasted their money. His melancholy descriptions of Alaska's climate and resources were his own opinions.

Too enamored of the fur seals to take stock of the Territory's less conspicuous latent resources, he saw Alaska's wealth concentrated in the two small islands lying two hundred miles from the mainland. Fulfilling his destiny as interpreter of the furred Alaskan treasure he had discovered, he lectured and wrote paeans to his wondrous animals. His original report, expanded and printed in the Tenth Census publications of 1880, was republished as a separate monograph a year or two later, and, in 1886, Charles Scribner's Sons published his *Our Arctic Providence, or Alaska and the Seal Islands.* Arrogantly Elliott disparaged his predecessors, even Steller. Condescendingly he wrote: "Considering the physical difficulties that environed Steller, the notes made by him on the sea-bears of the North Pacific are remarkably good; but . . . they fall so far from giving a fair and adequate idea of what these herds are and do as to be absolutely valueless for the present hour."

Elliott—and his fur seals—would pay dearly for his conceit, especially his failure to imitate Steller's caution. Hale and alert, victim of neither scurvy nor delusions of grandeur when he made his Bering Island studies, Steller commented, "If I were asked to state how many [fur seals] I have seen on Bering Island, I can say without lying that it is impossible to make any computation. They are innumerable." Ridicule of Elliott's census and the enumeration system that he insisted was the infallible yardstick of seal life was to cast doubt on the total number of victims of the catastrophe which was, even then, overtaking his fur seals.

12

No Man's Property

The Alaska Commercial Company's investment to popularize the sea bear's fur boomeranged to destroy the source of its profits. As soon as the fashionable ladies of the world adopted the smart fur seal sacque, a reign of terror struck the Pacific and the Bering Sea, a holocaust known as "pelagic sealing."

Pelagic sealing began when the first aboriginal hunter speared a fur seal from his canoe. For hundreds of years, bone-tipped or stone-tipped spears and harpoons provided littoral tribes with food, clothing, and oil for heat and light, without damaging the sea bear clans. Then, almost in a single season, it became an industry of civilized man, and desolation spread throughout the northern seal kingdom.

Modern pelagic sealing began off the coast of Washington and Vancouver Island before the Pribilof seals became Americans. A Canadian trader, Hugh Mackay, was persuaded by Indians from whom he bought furs, to ship them and their gear to the seal routes to avoid the risks of sea voyages in frail canoes. So successful was his trial trip in 1866 that, because his sloop *Ino* could carry only three canoes, he built the schooner *Favorite* solely for sealing. Other traders pioneered as seal fishers. Lest news of their profits attract competition, they were so closemouthed about their doings that only four or five schooners are known to have been sealing in that vicinity in 1879. Undoubtedly there were many more.

93

As the market for whale oil and whalebone narrowed and whales grew scarce, between 1872 and 1879, disappointed whalers stopped off to recoup their losses with a few hundred seal pelts stolen from unguarded Pribilof rookeries. Large-scale outfitting of ships for sealing voyages began, probably, in 1879. The following summer pelagic sealing emerged from its chance beginnings as a flourishing, established industry. Representing a large investment of capital, it provided work for shipbuilders; trade outlets for food, clothing, and other merchandise as well as employment for mariners and hunters. Largely replacing Indian sealers, schooner crews were recruited from the lawless flotsam of the seaports, the sea wolves whom Jack London depicted, men inured to hardships and dangerous toil, unafraid to clash with law officers.

Waiting for migrating seals off the coast of Washington in February, the schooners followed them northward. To get a satisfactory catch as more ships entered the chase, schooners pursued the seals through Aleutian passes into the Bering Sea, to the shores of their breeding islands. From a known total of 16 schooners in 1879, the sealing fleet by 1883 had increased to 34; in 1889 there were 115 fur pirates harrying the fur seals from Cape Flattery to the Pribilof Islands and beyond. A catch of 15,000 pelts reported in market lists of 1882 rose to 60,000 a year by 1895. Marked by spear tear or bullet hole, pelagic skins were easily distinguished from the undamaged ones of Pribilof or Asiatic seals killed on land by clubbing. London furriers referred to these torn, less valuable furs as "the Northwest Catch."

Mortality among fur seals was far more devastating than sale totals indicated. By the pelagic hunters' own admissions, the 15,000 furs sent to London in 1882 represented pelts recovered from between 120,000 to 150,000 slain animals. Since the majority of those killed at sea were pregnant females, the fatalities of the unborn were catastrophic, too.

Hundreds of pelagic sealers' affidavits frankly described the extent of their spoilation: the place and manner of killings, the elusiveness of their swimming targets, the abrupt sinkings of wounded seals, and the enormous wastage of seal life. Shamelessly they pictured the shambles of a schooner's deck at skinning time. Prematurely ripped from their dead or dying mothers by the skinners' cruel blades, tremulous viable fetuses stumbled blindly in the slippery white and crimson ooze of their mother's milk and blood smeared thickly over the planks. These terrible living unborn cried in anguished terror until a merciful foot kicked them overboard to drown.

Fur pirates candidly admitted their killings would soon exterminate the Pribilof fur seals. Attempting, as owner of their birthplaces, to end seal persecution at sea, the United States rashly ventured beyond traditional legality into untried diplomatic courses. Without warning either Great Britian or Canada or seeking their assistance in curbing their citizens, the Treasury Department impulsively ordered revenue steamers to apprehend sealing schooners—no matter which flags they flew, convoy them to Alaskan ports, and hand them over to an American District Court.

In 1886, after the U.S.S. *Corwin* had escorted three Canadian schooners to Sitka, Great Britain protested sharply to the Secretary of State, Mr. Bayard. The British note may have been Bayard's first intimation of the policy initiated by the Treasury. Pleading ignorance, he apologized he must study the undelivered reports of the *Corwin,* still patrolling the north, and the court transcripts. Sir Lionel Sackville-West, the British Minister in Washington, Earl of Iddesleigh and later the Marquis of Salisbury, impatiently pressed the untitled Mr. Bayard to explain the highhanded, inexplicable interference with the normal business of Englishmen.

Bayard repeated his early excuses. He also had to consult the Attorney General about his Government's attitude toward Bering Sea sovereignty, skirting the admission that the United States considered the Bering a *mare clausum,* as much its property as any harbor indenting its coast, and a part of its Alaskan Purchase. The basis for such a claim was the extraordinary boundary cited in the Treaty of Transfer, an imaginary line in the Bering Sea, running along the 193° of west longitude between Russia and Alaska, a piece of absurd diplomatic carelessness because the Czar's attempt to make the Bering a private Russian lake and bar other countries' shipping from its waters had been frustrated by England and the United States, a frustration solemnized by treaty in 1825.

Forewarned at least twice that the problem of protecting her peculiar mobile property at sea would have to be settled someday, conflicting opinions of responsible statesmen had prevented the United States from formulating a policy before a crisis arose—and continued to do so. When Chief Collector Phelps of the San Francisco Customs office reported, in 1872, that ships were getting ready in many harbors, including Honolulu and Australian ports, to go seal fishing near the Pribilofs, Secretary of the Treasury Boutwell stated: "I do not see that the United States would have the jurisdiction or power to drive off parties going up there for that purpose unless they made such attempts within a marine league of shore." But, faced with a similar warning from the Collector of Customs in San Francisco ten years later, Acting Secretary of the Treasury, Mr. French, cited the unique longitudinal Alaskan boundary set forth in the treaty: "All waters within that boundary to the western end of the Aleutian Archipelago and chain of islands are considered as comprised within the waters of Alaskan Territory." Only north of the Aleutians, within those longitudinal boundaries, did the revenuers interfere with sealing schooners. In domestic councils, defenders of traditional freedom of the seas and fur seal partisans tried vainly to hammer out a sensible policy. Judged by official acts, most policy makers of President Cleveland's first administration considered the treaty boundary valid.

When the owners of the *Corwin's* captives, the Canadian *Onward, Carolina,* and *Thornton,* were tried in the District Court at Sitka in 1886, Judge Dawson, after consultation with the Attorney General, described the boundary set forth in the treaty and instructed the jury that if they believed the accused had killed any marine furred animals in the Bering Sea east of 193° west longitude, they "should find the defendants guilty." The vessels were condemned. Belligerent notes arrived from London. In the interest of peace, Mr. Bayard happily informed the London foreign office in the following February, 1887, that President Cleveland had freed men and vessels. It was, the British assumed, a full retreat. Queen Victoria and her lion relaxed, but the Canadians were nervous.

Within a few weeks the British asked for guarantees that Canadian vessels, sailing out as usual to seal, would not be molested. In a series of ingenious replies, Mr. Bayard guaranteed nothing. The Canadian fleet entered the Bering Sea. American patrols arrested three schooners. The British protest arrived promptly. Acknowledging its receipt, Mr. Bayard produced his stereotyped excuse—lack of information.

Trenchantly the British called attention to the 1824-25 treaties with the Czar, quoting John Quincy Adams to embarrass the Americans. Bayard sidestepped the issue by instigating a discussion to define the scope of the phrase "the Pacific Ocean." Wrangling over the status of the Bering as a separate sea or as an arm of the Pacific befuddled diplomatic exchanges, while American statesmen sought a way to preserve their fur seals and international comity. In the late summer of 1887 Secretary Bayard invited England, Russia, Japan, France, Germany, Sweden, and Norway to frame a convention restraining their nationals from pelagic sealing. Minister Phelps in London predicted success for this belated American appeal for co-operation. Lord Salisbury, displaying open sympathy for the fur seals, agreed to postpone discussion of the Bering's status until after the convention and requested a copy of America's conservation proposals. Unprepared for such swift acquiescence, Bayard presented the proposals late the next February, 1888.

The United States proposed a closed season during which nations accepting the regulations would restrain their citizens from pelagic sealing with guns, spears, or nets from April 1 to

November 1 above 50° north latitude and from the Pacific
Coast to 180° west longitude. Bayard reminded Lord Salisbury
of England's economic stake in the Pribilof fur seals—the ten
thousand London fur workers whose livelihood depended on
the fur seals. He also promised Salisbury, in a private letter to
Minister Phelps, that no Canadian vessels would be arrested
during the conversations. No public announcement of this recess
was possible in 1888, a presidential election year, lest the Republicans make too much capital of the incumbent Democrats'
apparent capitulation to the English Crown. Complaining that
previous orders to revenue ships had not been rescinded, the
Canadians would not comply with Salisbury's request to refuse
their sealers clearance papers. By the time Washington explained that no orders to make arrests had been issued that
season, the only means of accomplishing noninterference without rousing public opinion, the Canadians were hunting in the
north with no hovering revenuer to stay their killings.

Russia and Japan, owners of the home islands of the two
Asiatic branches of the seal family, accepted Bayard's invitation. Disclaiming commercial interest in fur seals, other countries declined. Russia proposed that the whole Bering Sea and
the Okhotsk Sea be declared out of bounds during the closed
season; Japan, that sea otter hunting also be outlawed. Abruptly
giving way to Canadian obduracy, Salisbury withdrew from
negotiations. In turn, the discouraged State Department
brusquely canceled the conference with Japan and Russia.

All during the summer of 1888 Bayard solicited further talks
with Salisbury, but the British demurred and procrastinated
until a new crisis agitated diplomatic offices: the advertisement
of the sale of four vessels seized in the Bering in 1887. Bargaining for English acquiescence to further talks, Bayard offered to
release the schooners to owners who posted bond until their
cases were reviewed by an American court. The nominal owners of the *Grace, Dolphin,* and *Anna Berg* demanded lower
bonds. Registered as Canadian vessels, they were almost wholly
American-owned. American poachers concealed their partici-

pation in sealing because their hunting ran counter to general
public feeling. No owner appeared to protest seizure or sale of
the *Ada,* a mystery ship—her clearance papers from Shanghai.
Canadian authorities finally informed Great Britain her anonymous owner would not contest the bond. Appraisal arguments
dragged on for months. The vessels deteriorated; the cost of
guarding them mounted. The year ended with diplomatic mis-
sives about the boats' value crisscrossing the Atlantic from Ot-
tawa to London to Washington and back again. No compromise was reached. The following March the vessels were sold.
Bayard's bargaining had been fruitless.

Long before that sale, more serious friction, growing out of
America's slowly maturing resolve to protect her property at
any cost, overshadowed the boat dispute. In the autumn of
1888 Minister Phelps advised the State Department to relinquish all hope of immediate, amicable settlement and to adopt
one of the only alternatives he could envisage: either permit the
Pribilof herd to be exterminated, or harass seal poachers until
loss of income and property forced Great Britain and Canada
to regulate pelagic hunting. Maritime law had always been
amended by events—he cited changes introduced to stop the
slave trade. Problems rising from the fur seals' dual existence
must be solved by similar pressure of necessity, since the United
States had a valid, legal claim to animals born on her soil and
spending at least a third of their lives ashore on their birthrocks.
Even though the extinction of the seals would throw thousands
of London fur workers out of jobs that had paid them more than
$21,000,000 since 1867, pleas of influential British furriers,
such as Lampson and Son, vigorously pressed since 1886, had
been of no avail. To maintain prestige as guardian of her colonies, Great Britain would have to sacrifice the Londoners' livelihood and welfare to support the temporary interests of a much
smaller number of Canadian subjects.

Legislators were as discouraged as Phelps when Congress,
that same fall, examined the "Bering Sea Question." Cautious
legislators voted down hotheaded representatives in the House

who wanted an immediate proclamation of American adherence to the longitudinal Alaskan boundary.

In the closing hours of Cleveland's administration, a bill was pushed through Congress ordaining a presidential proclamation to restrain hunting and fishing in the Bering within "the domain of the United States." Its authors termed the innocuously worded clause authorizing the President to maintain patrol vessels in the Bering to protect American interests, a mere reminder of existing Executive powers. The new English Minister, Sir Julian Pauncefote, relayed gossip to London that the bill passed so late in the evening that it reached Cleveland after midnight, after he had ceased to be President, and he had deliberately signed it under a false Saturday date line. That the upright Cleveland would have stooped to such trickery, even to save seal lives, was a ridiculous notion. But the very authorization of a presidential proclamation, however vague, antagonized the British. The United States was obviously determined to protect Pribilof seals. But how—and more important— where? American replies to requests for definition of the phrase, "the domain of the United States," were not illuminating. The *Rush* left San Francisco May 24, to patrol the Bering, followed shortly by the *Bear*. British queries were answered by events: the cutters began to pick up poachers in the Bering outside the three-mile limit.

Believing an American-born seal as entitled to protection on the high seas as an American citizen, the public and the press upheld their Government's stand—legal or illegal, they cared not. Adverse criticism was limited almost wholly to letter columns. In the New York *Evening Post*, in June, Professor Robert Rayner asserted that, even if the "seals were all American-born, it would make no difference in law," as "creatures roaming about the high seas are no man's property, except his who catches them." A pamphlet, brought out by C. D. Ladd in San Francisco, contained many constructive proposals, mere padding around a "closed season," Ladd, as owner of one and possibly more pelagic schooners, desired. Whether honest opinion or cunning propaganda of pelagic sealers, all public criticisms of national policy were quoted to trip up Bayard and his successor, Mr. Blaine.

War and rumors of war crept into the newspapers and conversations of Americans, Canadians, and Englishmen that summer of 1889. Encounters in the Bering were practice engagements. Only fur seal blood was flowing; the threat of human bloodshed was real. Two incidents afforded Canadians the delight of winning minor skirmishes. The *Black Diamond* encounter seemed a significant victory.

When the *Rush* overtook the *Black Diamond* and Captain Thomas refused a third hail to stop, the *Rush* steamed ahead and cut across the schooner's bow. Locking up his ship's papers, Thomas taunted Captain Shepherd, who headed the boarding party. But Shepherd forced the lock and took the documents. He also appropriated sealskins, guns, and Indian spears. Stationing a single American seaman aboard, he ordered Thomas to sail to Sitka and surrender to the American authorities. Undeterred by the presence of one American but unable to continue sealing without weapons, Thomas headed directly for Victoria, British Columbia, to be greeted as a national hero. Newspapers berated the United States for robbing this honest businessman of 10,000 furs. In his affidavit Thomas swore he lost only 131 salted skins.

The *Triumph* affair was similar. News of these "victories" winged to London, followed by reports of other schooners stopped, their skins and weapons confiscated, at times even their salt supply. The Canadians had too hastily presumed that a single seaman aboard a schooner indicated that United States resolution was faltering. The new tactics stopped sealing without the Americans having to convoy prizes to port, guard captured boats, or become entangled in court suits. The cutters remained on patrol duty. Confiscation of arms and supplies only too successfully disabled a schooner. Owners found themselves with few or no skins, disgruntled crews to pay off, many expenses and no income. Uncle Sam, they concluded, had thought up a devilish machination to ruin their business, but it was actually an expedient adopted by Revenue officers who lacked seamen to take captured schooners to Alaskan ports. The action was so detrimental to sealing that the infuriated, badly frightened Canadians prepared to defend their rights. Meanwhile Treasury officers were asking, If the Canadians armed, were there still fur seals to fight for?

13

Where Are the Fur Seals?

S O S, flashed Agent Goff from St. Paul Island to Washington in the autumn of 1889. The fur seals were almost gone; the retiring Company had been unlawfully killing undersized males. Stunned Washington officials read the news; an incredulous Elliott heard the tidings. Could such a stupendous loss occur in a single season? Had a gradual decrease never been reported by local custodians? Were Agent Goff's impressions exaggerated?

Blind to hints of ruinous changes in the annual Pribilof reports of the seal's welfare, Elliott had assumed that the threat to their existence at sea would be averted before the seal millions were disastrously affected: Goff's notice pierced the thick cocoon of unjustified confidence which had insulated him from even the suspicion that his animals were in actual jeopardy. In his favorite retreat, the little Tower Room at the Smithsonian, he pored anxiously over market lists of pelagic catches and the Pribilof agents' reports. Examined for indications of danger, both suggested perplexing questions which could not be answered until the seals came back to their beaches in the spring and were counted—by his own infallible system.

His own opinionated gullibility must have haunted him as he read and realized how his earlier belief in the imperishable, undamageable fecundity of the Pribilof herd and his unquestioning trust in their commercial wardens had blunted his abil-

ity to foresee the vicissitudes the seals had met. He must have
remembered that, because Professor Baird, a Smithsonian scientist, warned the information might arouse and guide greedy
men, he had suppressed in his monograph his opinion that a
small fleet of marine hunters could destroy the host in a few
seasons as they emerged from Aleutian passages into the Bering.

The stereotyped phrases of the agents' reports had an ugly
sound. Year after year, agent after agent had used the same
stock phrases: seal life not being depleted; no perceptible diminution; no trouble in filling the quota. Sour notes broke the
harmony occasionally.

Agents had frequently advised St. George quota changes.
Picturing the bachelors flitting restlessly from island to island,
Elliott had considered them natural. Had he been disposed to
worry over the census, his doubts would have been stilled in
1879 when Agent Morton, voluntarily applying the professor's
ignored system of seal counting, reported enlarged rookeries.
Yet Morton had doubted his own findings. As soon as the
Treasury Department acted on his report to increase the St.
George quota to 20,000, Morton feared to take more than
18,000. Veering toward optimism a few weeks later, he predicted St. George could supply 20,000 the next summer.

Submitting his first report in 1879, Agent Otis refrained from
a personal appraisal of the herd. The Aleuts insisted the herd
had declined seriously and blamed the newly installed blubber
refining plant for driving the seals away, a preposterous notion
according to experienced resident officials, commercial and
governmental, since fur seals were indifferent to disagreeable
odors. Otis pledged to make a careful investigation. By summer he was enrolled in the regular choir—no diminution of seal
life. What worth Aleut gossip—even their warnings—to protect
their fur seals?

Otis and his successor, Agent Glidden, faced new problems:
the lessees' demand to buy prime skins of seals killed for Aleut
food in addition to their quota, and their imperious request that
Aleuts be denied their "spring chicken," the several thousand

fat pups the sealers were allowed to kill each fall. Preferring conventional American dress, the Aleuts no longer used sealskin clothing, but made gloves, caps, blankets, and coats of them to barter to visiting seamen for trinkets or forbidden liquor. What had induced Company officers to worry so much about Aleut intemperance that they were willing to substitute corned beef and extra milk for the seal meat at Company expense? Pup killing ceased for a single season only. For the first time the Aleuts had rebelled successfully, a circumstance suspicious in itself, indicating that local authorities might have feared the damaging revelations of angry sealers. Had the forays of poachers, the shrunken rookery limits, or some other ominous symptom that the seals were disappearing, inspired the lessees' desire to acquire extra skins and to make sure all young seals matured?

When the Russian agent of the Commander and Robben Islands, Nicholas Grebnitzky, visited St. Paul in 1882, he boasted of the Asiatic herds' recovery from the murderous seasons of unwarded killing. During his 5 years in office, the annual catch had risen from 11,000 to 45,000 skins. On Robben Island, small and difficult to guard from sly visits of passing ships, the lessees had killed closely to prevent their property being stolen, but the rookery populations of Bering and Copper Islands once more numbered millions, thanks to careful husbandry and improved sealing techniques—not the advent of Pribilof seals. The Commander seals were noticeably different from their Pribilof relatives, as well as from the Kuril and Robben Island seals, he alleged. The head measurements were not the same; their furs not the same color or quality. Agent Wardman implied Grebnitzky's information should be passed on to Professor Elliott, who thought the Pribilof seals, if molested, might flee to the Commander Islands.

London market news alone should have alerted Elliott. To stabilize falling prices due to the influx of pelts from British Columbia, the lessees took only 75,000 skins in 1883, a season they had experienced the greatest difficulty in getting 15,000

St. George bachelors. Yet Agent Glidden sent the usual glib
news the fur seals were flourishing, at the same time suggesting
that the St. George quota be cut in half for 3 years.

Elliott's yardstick had been applied again on St. George in
1886 by Chief Agent Tingle. Substituting a larger average seal
because Elliott's hypothetical one seemed to him too small, he
announced an increase of a million St. George animals. His
survey the following year confirmed the high census. Since his
own, although amended, system disclosed no losses, Elliott had
continued to ignore the pelagic sealers—ten schooners were arrested in the Bering in 1886, and started corresponding amiably
with Tingle to persuade him his average seal was too large. The
lessees, however, put no trust in Tingle's census.

Elliott may not have known that, in 1889, the last year of
its franchise, the Alaska Commercial Company dispatched the
journalist, Theodore Williams, to examine every aspect of
open-sea sealing—its scope, its profits, its possible injury to
the herd—in order to make a "safe bid," to "offer the largest amount overlapping other competitors" without paying
more for the lease "than it was worth." Williams reported
frightful ravages and reckless waste of seal lives. Since seal
depletion worried Company directors, Treasury agents, too,
must have known and concealed the truth. Undoubtedly many,
interested only in the salary of a dull job on a lonely island,
had not been competent to judge the flux and ebb of seal
beaches, might not even have watched seal life season after
season. More informed agents, skeptical of the reception their
revelations would meet in Washington where the lessees had so
many powerful friends, might have feared to jeopardize their
jobs. Company officials could have deluded, frightened, or paid
Government personnel to conceal the ghastly truth. Whatever
the reasons, ignorance, indifference, or fear, Pribilof history
had, year by year, been falsely presented to the nation by its
own servants.

Most fatal of Elliott's youthful misjudgments had been his
infatuated admiration for Hayward Hutchinson, "that great-

hearted man," and, after his death, for Hutchinson's organization. Fatuous public compliments he paid Hutchinson had been no bids for personal attention and favors. He had genuinely idolized that bold, resourceful profit seeker and credited his Company with an integrity it did not merit. The loss of his illusion that the lessees' self-interest in the continuance of regular profits would be the animals' greatest protection, marked the beginning of Elliott's lifelong distrust of monopolies. Fur seal and fur seal expert had been betrayed by the Company's failure to sound the tocsin that the fur seals were dying. Others might be forgiven their crimes and mistakes—pelagic sealers, owners of death ships, fumbling diplomats, even indolent, venial Government agents—but not those who, entrusted with the source of fur seal fecundity, had permitted it to seep slowly away in secrecy, without attempting to stem the fatal flow. If Goff's report were true—and in December he sent fuller, more depressing details—the guilty man must be punished. Elliott would avenge the murdered seals.

Goff's December note advised a quota reduction to fifty thousand furs the next summer, urged the swift ejection of the fur pirates from the sealing waters, and pressed for immediate reforms in sealing methods on land: no more killing after July 20, when harem discipline began to relax, and cows wandered aimlessly over the beaches, frequently rounded up with the bachelors and killed by the sealing gang. Without careful examination the most experienced Aleuts could not distinguish between young males and females. If the herd were to recover, not another cow must die accidentally beneath a sealer's club or another pup become a sealer's dinner. The Government must consent to furnish sealers with food and other supplies if their income, proportionate to the quota, were to be cut in half.

So interwoven were the destinies of fur seals and sealers that it was not surprising the news, "the seals are not here," came accompanied by a medical report that the sealers, too, were disappearing. Company doctors had rarely furnished agents with more than bare vital statistics for their annual reports. As regularly each year as the statement that the fur seals were not perceptibly decreasing, another formula had gone to Washington: "The health of the Aleuts is generally good." No matter how many sealers died during the year—and most of them, according to some agents, died from "imprudence"—that bland refrain accompanied the death list. In this year of revelations, Dr. Lutz reported that the human death rate was 84 per 1,000. Artificially bolstered by 76 bridal immigrants from the Archipelago and their progeny, the 1889 census of 223 Aleuts was misleading. Unless swift assistance were forthcoming and the diet and living conditions of the sealers improved, they would follow their fur seals into oblivion.

A dying people and a dying animal, both victims of "imprudence" during the Alaska Commercial Company's reign, should have embarrassed the lessees' efforts to renew the lease. Either Treasury officers were not deeply shocked by the disclosures of Dr. Lutz and Agent Goff or they considered them exaggerated. Secretary Windom, in his report to Congress, asserted that the Alaska Commercial Company tenure had demonstrated the value of a faithfully administered leasing system, but he awarded the franchise to the North American Commercial Company, a newly organized corporation capitalized for $2,000,000. Perhaps the first lessees, cognizant of an inevitable reduction in profit, bid too cautiously. They may have relied too strongly on their Pribilof properties—the frame dwellings, storehouses, and sealing tackle—to establish their incontestable right to a new lease. But in 1890 the stratagem that Hutchinson had employed so skillfully at Sitka in 1867, failed.

The Alaska Commercial Company was believed to have averaged an annual profit of $1,000,000. In 18 years the national Treasury had received $8,000,000 from rent, taxes, and duty on dressed skins. Over $5,000,000 came from the Pribilof bachelors; $500,000 represented duty on imported Commander skins; another large portion the duty on skins which the lessees had purchased from pelagic sealers—the "Sand Point Catch." The Company had been not only an observer but a customer of the pelagic assassins! The maintenance of Pribilof agents and revenue steamers to guard the islands had cost about $500,000. The fur seals in 20 years had paid for the Territory of Alaska.

For its first season the new Company was tentatively allotted a quota of 60,000 skins; successive ones to be regulated by the Secretary of the Treasury. The annual rent was increased to $60,000. The tax on each skin shipped from the islands—the lessees never bore the loss of damaged skins—was raised to $9.62½. The increase of $7 was not excessive. In 1868 a salted pelt sold for only $2.50; in 1890, having become a fashionable luxury fur, it brought $30. Food allowances determined annually by the Treasury, 80 tons of coal a year, free dwellings —Hutchinson's precedent became an obligation to his successor—a church building, a school, teachers, and doctors—all these the new Company must provide the sealers. The new lessees paid a high price for Hutchinson's frame houses and began immediate expensive repairs in order that these should last their tenure.

No sooner had the North American Commercial Company won its franchise than ex-Government Agent Tingle accused a prominent officer and stockholder named Liebes of owning shares in a pelagic schooner. Under oath, officers of the new firm denied the accusation. Tingle quickly backed down. The lessees were restored to favor; their contract was safe. Two decades later, positive proofs of Liebes' actual pelagic connections, including his signature as part owner of a sealing schooner registered at the San Francisco Customs office, were exhumed by Elliott. Shortly after his about-face, in May, Tingle appeared on St. Paul as the new Company's superintendent. So inexplicable an appointment seemed to many a reward that Liebes and his associates had paid for withdrawal of his charges. Fearfully the sealers watched him land. As a Treasury agent he had been an arrogant bully, imposing extraordinarily heavy fines for minor disobediences. The most brutal overseer since the days of the *promyshlenniki,* he had even manacled offenders with leg irons and handcuffs. Powerless as a Company officer to inflict physical punishment, his contemptuous, abusive remarks—he even called the sealers monkeys—caused many unhappy incidents, even strikes, during his superintendency.

In February 1890 Elliott submitted to the Treasury the casualty list he had compiled during his winter studies, an estimate that pelagic sealers had killed 1½ million seals. He importuned the Department to heed Goff's storm warnings and let him ascertain the true state of Pribilof affairs. In view of his reputation, he was the Treasury's best candidate, but his urgings were misrepresented later by enemies as shameful chicanery to get a job. Duly appointed, he returned to the Pribilofs in the spring.

The spectacle of the seal beaches appalled him; some rookeries abandoned and grass-grown, others shrunken. Of the host which had captured his heart and imagination in 1872, a "scant million" survived. It was an awful hour when he stood once more on the stubby volcanic cone of Hutchinson Hill on Northeast Point and recalled his bewildered ecstasy when he had first looked down from there at the surging tide of animal life, many millions strong, fecund, virile, and magnificent. Now he saw lonely clusters of fur seals scattered along the shore. Lava boulders, burnished by the passage of millions of flippers of countless generations, gaped like raw welts between the huddled groups. Untenanted rocks accused him of murder. Not only lessees and sea pirates were culpable. He, the careless shepherd, had not watched his flock.

Barely a hundred thousand St. Paul bachelors hauled out. From the killers' own confessions, the acknowledged routes and time schedules of pirate schooners, Elliott knew that the swollen-bodied, slower-coursing gravid cows had been the pelagic hunters' chief victims. Where, then, were the bachelors? Had so many thousands been destroyed at sea? It did not seem to him that fetal casualties or food killings could account for the decrease. He studied the islands' logs, the daily records of seal drives for the preceding twenty years. He cross-examined the sealers. Worthless as public proof of malpractice, certain to be denied in the presence of their island bosses, their answers enlightened him. They told of barbarous tactics that Company managers employed when bachelors were scarce. To drive them permanently from inaccessible shore rims, the rocks had been strewn with broken glass and rubbish. Small bands, loafing too close to the sea to be surrounded, had been stampeded by the clamor of shrill police whistles—the sealers wore them tucked under their shirts, Elliott discovered. The St. Paul log showed cause for such cruelty.

Until 1877 the lessees' quota had been filled from a few hauling grounds; thereafter the hunters had to invade every nook and corner of the seal beaches. Then the captives had been marched mercilessly, some for miles, along an extended, rugged, rock-strewn course to the regular killing fields. Rejected seals had probably been driven over and over that tortuous, exhaustive passage—since there were no longer undisturbed and peaceful beaches on which they might hide. Elliott leaped to the conclusion that the frequently repeated, violent exertions must have devitalized the future fathers of the species and have destroyed their virility. The greedy lessees had not only concealed the awful losses of pelagic hunting but had maltreated and abused male refugees who had run the sea gantlet safely. Legally responsible for the seals, they had betrayed the nation's trust and were more guilty than the sea killers. They shared, with the latter, the blame for the murder of over four million seals.

Elliott and the resident Treasury agents, headed by Goff, watched the daily roundup of small bands of males. By July 20, when the harems had begun to disperse, only 21,000 had been executed—barely more than a third of the quota. Upheld by Elliott, Agent Goff ordered killing stopped. Superintendent Tingle ignored the fact that Goff had recommended that terminal sealing date the previous year. Repudiating his previous fervent admiration for the expert, he singled out Elliott as the villain who perverted the judgment of sensible Government officials. Since fine young males were arriving daily, Elliott was not

merely defrauding the lessees, raged Tingle. The sealers would
starve. The Company need not support them unless its sealing
income covered the expense.

Tingle might bully Aleuts, but not Elliott and Goff. Assistant
agents backed them up, confident that when the authority's
report reached Washington, Tingle and his crowd would learn
they could not gamble with seal lives.

Elliott's demands were radical and uncompromising: immediate suspension of land killing for at least seven years, payment
of enough compensation for pelagic hunters' losses to obtain a
conservation treaty that would forever end seal persecution at
sea, and, if compensation were not enough, division of future
Pribilof profits with the British. The "seal life candle" should
no longer burn at both ends—the animals be destroyed on land
and at sea. He, the expert, would extinguish the consuming
fires.

But it was Elliott's flaming indictment that shocked decorous
Government circles, and was extinguished. Affrighted officials
read his denunciations and hastily transferred Agent Goff to a
Canadian customs post and excluded the "Professor" from important conferences. Instead of producing incontrovertible evidence that fur seals were America's exclusive property, his
scathing condemnation of monopolistic land management was
more vitriolic than his censure of pelagic sealing. He was attacking the basic principles of private enterprise. His proposed
sealing recess seemed Utopian folly to the Company's officers
and their friends in office. It was ridiculous to think the British
would be impressed by a *zapusk*. The Canadians would jeer
and catch more seals. Should they enrich themselves while
Americans lost money? His written word could be suppressed
but Elliott himself could not be easily silenced; his reputation
as the fur seal authority was incontestable. Nevertheless, rumors, contradictory and vicious, spread rapidly throughout
Washington. He was, at one and the same moment, the tool
of the Alaska Commercial Company, a British agent and a
hireling of Canadian pirates.

An Elephant Seal

(*Above*) Steller's Sea Lions, St. Paul Island

(*Below*) A Pod of Pribilof Bachelors

The strange furred creatures of land and sea had appropriately selected a strange personality to rescue them from jeopardy. He had truly been a doomed young man when he rode into their kingdom in 1872. Camped out on the edge of Washington, he subordinated all personal interests to the defense of his fur seals. A Don Quixote jousting at many windmills, but sometimes sending his point home to the very heart of ruthless commerce and organized greed, he was to be, from that summer of 1890 to his life's end, the fur seals' loyal, though most imperfect, knight.

14

Hearths and Pockets

On a September evening in 1889, vociferous Canadians crowded a meeting, presided over by the Mayor, in Victoria's city hall. Called to consider ways and means of protecting the pelagic sealing industry, the assembly became a challenge to the neighbor south of their border, a reproach to Great Britain for supine appeasement, and a demonstration for war.

American seizures affected not only "individual pockets and the province" but "our hearts," the first speaker began. The British Empire had been attacked, its flag trampled in the dust. Demonstrators abused the British navy for letting foreign enemies attack Canadian boats at sea. Like his predecessor, Lord Beaconsfield, Salisbury could assert, "I have kept the peace" but not add "with honor," having avoided war "at the sacrifice of the liberty of the greatest and most war-like nation in the world." War was terrible, a member of the Canadian Parliament admitted; peace preserved by the loss of national honor more terrible. Too long Brother Jonathan had been twisting the tail of the British lion with impunity. The hour had struck for the "simple fishermen of Victoria" to light a lucifer under the lethargic old animal's nose. Moderate speakers argued arbitration, "from a dollar-and-cent point of view," must be immediate. Cheers and cries of "That's right!" greeted the most belligerent diatribes. If Great Britain did not protect their interests at once, the Victoria fishermen would substitute guns for diplomacy. The meeting's inflammatory resolutions roused the British lion. Sir Julian Pauncefote asked Secretary Blaine to reopen negotiations.

There must be a truce by April, Blaine warned, if there were to be seals to protect by arbitration. Both diplomats agreed protective fur seal regulations would erase the question of Bering Sea jurisdiction. Let the Americans publicly abandon such claims, Canada, still rattling the sealers' sword, declaimed. Her delegate must be a member of the proposed commission; she must ratify all agreements. Blaine curtly dismissed her demands. Canada's Privy Council turned down Salisbury's appeals for moderation and warned him that, since the Dominion's Fisheries Department had decided killer whales destroyed more seals than human hunters, and only one per cent of the seals killed in the water were lost, no proposal for a closed season would be entertained.

Pauncefote passed Canada's opinions and ultimatums on to Blaine in the deadline month of April 1890, and, later, her gestures of friendship as he defined her murderous sealing scheme, alleged conservation proposals. Most outrageous was a ten-mile safety zone around the Pribilofs in summer. Treasury Agent Taylor was quoted to support the murder trap which all seals, except bulls and pups confined to the rookeries, but especially pregnant nursing mothers, would enter to feed. Speculating that females might go ten or fifteen miles or even farther from the islands for fish, Taylor confessed he did "not know the average of it." The pelagic sealers, however, did know.

Blaine immediately rejected what he termed a hunting schedule designed to enable poachers to exterminate the fur seals in two or three seasons. "The respect which the sealing vessels would pay to the ten-mile limit would be the same wolves pay to a flock of sheep so placed that no shepherd can guard them." The two nations finally agreed to arbitrate after a joint commission of experts had studied the fur seals. Efforts to halt pelagic sealing that summer and until the conflict was settled by arbitration foundered in a series of acrimonious notes.

Blaine transmitted six points he and President Harrison wanted settled by arbitration to Lord Salisbury in December. Five maintained the U.S. right to protect her Pribilof herd. The last, formulation of pelagic sealing rules, would depend on the arbitrators' resolution of the first five.

It was February (1890) when Salisbury responded. He took exception only to certain clauses, particularly the statement that American ownership of the seals' birthplaces vested the United States with title to the animals themselves. Conservation regulations were matters which would "more fitly form the substance of a separate reference." He was certain President Harrison would "be very glad to repair" an important omission, indemnity for seized sealing schooners. Intent on ending pelagic sealing and devoid of imperial ambitions to rule over the Bering Sea, American diplomats did not realize how subtly the British were shifting emphasis from the seals to Bering Sea sovereignty, and welcomed partial approbation as a real concession. Their satisfaction was short-lived.

Unexpectedly the British requested the absolute suspension of land sealing if a joint proclamation were to stay the poachers at sea. Some American newspapers thought the request reasonable; others denounced it. The British, many Americans grumbled, were as daft as Elliott. Why should Americans stop killing their own seals? Furthermore, the contract with the lessees was inviolable. The American most deeply offended by this demand seems to have been Senator Elkins, who had been campaign manager for Blaine's unsuccessful presidential try in 1884 and had nominated and campaigned in behalf of President Harrison. It was natural that Elkins should hurry down to Washington to see those two good friends in April, the month the Company's sealing preparations should start, when, as a stockholder in the North American Commercial Company, he learned its sealing rights were threatened. The *New York Times* stated, "Mr. Blaine, by his delays and his influence, succeeded in doing his friends of the North American Commercial Company a very substantial service after all." A letter to the press about this private friendly visit, signed Henry Wood Elliott, embarrassed clandestine plans for friendly favors, but Harrison abruptly introduced the Aleuts into the negotiations. Since the Company was obliged by its contract to provide for the sealers only out of income derived from sealing, at least enough animals to feed them must be killed.

Great Britain and the United States jointly proclaimed, on June 15, a *modus vivendi* for the fur seals for the remainder of the summer. On land, 7,500 seals were to be killed for Aleut food. Each nation appointed two scientists to the Bering Sea Commission to examine the fur seals' situation. Sir George Smyth Baden-Powell, brother of the renowned Boy Scout sponsor, and Professor Dawson, a Canadian geologist, represented Great Britain; Professor Mendenhall and Dr. Merriam, the United States.

While the Commissioners explored the Seal Islands, diplomats resumed efforts to define the remaining quarrels to be arbitrated. Indemnities roused most bitter debate. The United States desired compensation for all pelagic skins ever sent to market. Great Britain stood firm behind Canada's demand to be recompensed for inactivity during the *modus vivendi* as well as for property seizures. Her subjects were not idle, but during the summer no word of their exploits drifted south. Instead came an alarm that the lessee had illegally slaughtered nearly 10,000 Pribilof bachelors. Having already killed—and eaten— over 2,000 seals before June 15, the Aleuts, according to the resident agent, needed more meat. The treaty authorized killing 7,500 seals after its publication. While agreeing the interpretation was legal, British Commissioners had hurriedly notified their superiors of the extra killing. Sensibly the two nations decided not to quarrel over the death of a few more seals.

Behind the scenes, competing interests on both sides were applying relentless pressure and pulling strings which produced new perplexities. Lord Salisbury complained that all efforts to save fur seals would be futile if a third nation began pelagic sealing. Since scarcely six vessels of other countries had tried sealing in its first flourishing decade, and none had persisted, their own contemplated agreement should effectively discourage new entrants, the Americans argued. The Marquis relaxed when Blaine promised that their conclusions would be submitted to all maritime powers for ratification.

President Harrison hurried the negotiations. The United States—and the North American Commercial Company—could endure no more losses. The Americans quickly acceded to England's request the tribunal consist of seven judges instead of five: two representatives for each contestant; one neutral jurist of international reputation selected by France, Sweden, and Italy, respectively—all of them conversant with the English language. The last quibble had been ironed out; a joint memorandum signed by Blaine and Pauncefote drawn up. The treaty providing formally for arbitration was signed in February 1892, ratified by the Senate, and proclaimed May 9th. The fur seals had won an international court trial.

The preceding autumn had seen disquieting developments. Schooners came sailing back to Victoria with at least ten thousand pelts aboard from fresh sealing grounds west of the longitudinal boundary decreed by the *modus vivendi,* from the haunts of the Kuril and Commander fur seals. Never before 1891 had a flotilla of seal craft hunted the Asiatic herds, although whalers, fishermen, and sealers had visited their sea routes occasionally and raided their rookeries. The *modus vivendi* for Pribilof seals sentenced their Asiatic relatives to death. Next season, the Canadians brought back 25,000 furs; American poachers at least a quarter of that total. Despite edicts of the Czar and seizure of poachers by Russian naval vessels, depredations in the western Bering continued. England agreed to a temporary *modus vivendi* with Russia and made a formal gesture of assistance to the perishing Asiatic seals by sending a single patrol vessel into the myriad branching seal routes of the western Bering. After 1896 the catch declined because the Asiatic seals, like their Pribilof relatives, were dying. The self-destructive industry seemed to be expiring, and with it, all the northern fur seals. To many persons their extinction seemed the only peaceful solution to the Bering Sea dispute.

During preliminary talks begun in February 1892, in Washington, the four Commissioners found only two points of agreement: the Pribilof herd had been seriously damaged; the harm had been inflicted by human agents. The British blamed the first lessees' unchecked land killing; the Americans, the pelagic sealers, insisting land sealing had been carefully restricted and harmless to fur seal fertility. Elliott scornfully blasted the Commission's page and a half joint report: "This absurd mouse ran out from that laboring joint-commission . . . ," a mouse partly fattened on his own opinions. Unable to deny their request, a copy of his unprinted 1890 report had been furnished the British who, able to close their minds to his diatribes against pelagic sealing, found his wrathful indictment of the Alaska Commercial Company's sealing invaluable support for their viewpoint.

On both sides of the Atlantic the Commissioners' public utterances provoked ill feeling. The State Department censured the British Commissioners because their speeches revealed that even before they had seen one living fur seal, they were convinced pelagic sealing was harmless. In an apology spiced with malice, Minister Pauncefote declared that Americans, unfamiliar with the English language and idioms, had misunderstood the comments. Might he use the opportunity to convey his sympathy for America's dismal outlook at the arbitration hearings? How unfortunate that the publicly expressed opinions of the American Commissioners differed so from the Englishmen's conclusions, but they were, like their British colleagues, "honorable" men. Worn down after years of bickering, suave diplomatic tempers were fraying.

The outlook for its future was ominous when the fur seal set out for Paris to seek a reprieve. Professor Huxley, the English biologist, summarized the only alternatives: "One is to let the fur seals be extirpated. Mankind will not suffer much if the ladies are obliged to do without sealskin jackets; and the fraction of the English, Canadian, and American populations which lives on the sealskin industry will be no worse off than the vastly greater multitude who have had to suffer for the vagaries of fashion times out of number. Certainly if the seals are to be a source of constant bickering between two nations, the sooner they are abolished the better. The other course is to tread down all merely personal and trade interest in pursuit of an arrangement that will work and be fair all around: and to sink all the stupidities of national vanity and political self-seeking along with them. There is a great deal too much of all these undeniable elements apparent in the documents I have been studying."

The diplomatic adversaries were deaf to moderate suggestions. Elliott's proposal for total suspension of seal killing with compensation to the profit-seeking killers, and Huxley's were pushed aside. Too many individual pockets on both sides of the dispute clamored to be filled.

15

The Fur Seal Visits Paris

Arriving in Paris in the early spring of 1893 to plead for its life and the continuation of its species, the fur seal departed from French shores in midsummer under sentence of death. The judges pronounced a verdict deadly as a sealer's rifle. Human justice—biased, confused, fallible—ordained that the fur seal face continued slaughter on land and increasing peril, legal and inescapable, along its favorite seaways. One halfhearted gesture of defense was registered, a suggestion appended to the Award that, in view of the serious reduction the fur seal race had suffered from circumstances "not fully known," a total prohibition of land and sea killing for a period of two or three years, or even a single year, was advisable, and, if beneficial, should be repeated. Baron de Courcel, President of the arbitration court, and Supreme Justice Harlan, an American arbitrator, were the only judges to approve this advice.

As the Arbitration Treaty directed, each contestant delivered printed copies of its case to the judges and each other. Dismissing the seals as *ferae naturae,* wild animals no one could claim as property, masterless creatures on the high seas, the British took the initiative and made Bering Sea jurisdiction the pivotal, crucial issue. American attempts to keep seal problems paramount were frustrated. The freedom of the seas was at stake, the British argued. The judges must decide if a particular in-

121

dustry or animal excused a nation's interference with the human race's right to navigate on or fish in the high seas.

Instead of combating England's strategy resourcefully, the State Department and John W. Foster, special agent to handle arbitration protocol, only questioned British silence about the fur seal's peculiar nature and habits, which bore out the United States' claim to the animals as her property. Such information would be pertinent, replied Great Britain, only if the Tribunal decided concurrent regulations for preserving the fur seal were necessary. Otherwise the fur seal need not even enter the testimony until the United States had lost its case. The Court ordered the British Government to produce their Commissioners' findings and their conclusions, so hostilely detrimental to the fur seal's future.

The United States barely escaped the shame of bringing perjured testimony to court. Translations and photolithographs of purported Russian-Alaskan documents containing straightforward assertions of Russia's rule of the Bering as her private sea, historical precedents which would vindicate American actions against sealing schooners, were already printed in her countercase when Foster, for reasons he never explained, engaged a translator to determine their accuracy. Not one clause that strengthened the American position appeared in the originals. Confronted with true translations, Ivan Petroff, an irregularly employed U.S. Government interpreter, confessed he had fabricated the testimony to ingratiate himself with officials in order to secure the permanent office of curator of the Russian-American archives. So naïve an excuse for such an elaborate, expensive fraud evoked the suspicion that Petroff had been handsomely paid to discredit U.S. probity. The deceit uncovered before the American case was dismissed for misrepresentation, Foster immediately furnished the Court and his opponents with printed corrections. Whatever sinister backstage forces manipulated Petroff, their knavery was balked.

The English countercase was less reply to American claims than a body of fresh accusations, delivered so close to the expiration of the period allotted for replies that the United States could not secure rebuttal privileges. Protesting its contents were unjust, the President and American diplomats, pressed by the North American Commercial Company's political friends, permitted the arbitration to proceed.

The Tribunal met briefly in February and again in March to receive the printed arguments. At a third sitting, on April 4th, the British counsel requested a copy of Elliott's 1890 report. Although the Treaty forbade the introduction of further evidence after the counterarguments had been submitted, the refusal to produce a document already familiar to the English Commissioners might seem an admission that the United States feared Elliott's judgments. Under protest, the United States waived its right of refusal, stipulating only that the report's contents be available to both parties. A British attempt to present further evidence after the March 23rd recess was thwarted.

Oral arguments, opened on April 12th, continued, 4 hours a day, 4 days a week, until July 8th. Mr. Carter and Mr. Coudert opened the hearings with an exposition of the U.S. case. The Attorney General of England, Sir Richard Webster, and Mr. Robinson, a Canadian lawyer, presented the English point of view. Genuinely convinced his cause was just, that old protagonist of America's bold interference with pelagic offenders, former Minister Phelps, summarized American contentions.

Although their hopes of winning unusual jurisdictional rights in the Bering Sea were slight, American advocates had never doubted that their claim Pribilof fur seals were national property, therefore their responsibility on land or sea, would be denied by an impartial court. Aware of the novelty of their premise, they still were confident the legal definition of property would cover an animal which spent a third of its life on American soil, its birthplace. But, early in the proceedings, the Americans discovered that their opponents had compiled from the written or published utterances of American citizens weighty and telling contradictions to their every postulate and embarrassing evidence that their conduct as seal owners had been most reprehensible. The United States' position appeared absurd and untenable.

Suing for international recognition of her vested rights in Pribilof seals wherever they roamed and unwilling to spare their lives on their home islands, the United States' demand that other nations suffer commercial losses and co-operate to conserve American property seemed outrageously egotistical and inconsistent.

"The subject has become a weariness," said Mr. Phelps, opening his summation on the forty-third day of the hearings. In the main the arguments had been a repetition of all the claims and counterclaims, protests and controversies, that had filled diplomatic dispatches for nine years—with one significant change. Formerly Lord Salisbury believed the fur seal faced extinction. Now British advocates insisted they were not really being exterminated, but, if they were, the cause was indiscriminate land killing, not sea hunting. They insinuated that the lessees had exceeded their quota. They emphasized the waste of young seal life, the 129,530 pups killed during 20 years for Aleut food, 7 per cent of the quota. Magnifying Elliott's criticisms of land sealing and the derelictions of Treasury Agents, ugly facts of the United States' failure to watch over animals she called her exclusive property, were mercilessly bared. Quotations from American pelagic sealers' propaganda undermined their country's case. The British presented a masterly defense of pelagic sealing as the legitimate natural development of Indian hunting, censuring land killings as unnatural, unsporting, a savage pastime compared to fox hunting. At sea the fur seal enjoyed a fox's privilege, a chance to flee its pursuers.

American attorneys could not deny that the Treasury agents' unvaried generalizations about the Pribilof herd had satisfied its Federal guardians; that the latter had ignored all constructive suggestions to safeguard the seals. Following Maynard's advice to make an annual seal count, even if Elliott's method were imperfect, would have been proof America was keeping track of her seals. Quoting from Elliott's 1890 report, the British twisted his angry attacks on the lessees to strangle the animal's defense. No one mentioned his strictures against pelagic sealing or his program for sealing reform. Unable to rid himself of the Elliott incubus, Phelps even admitted excessive seal driving in 1890, an emergency expedient due to the scarcity of bachelors that season, which Elliott had mistakenly accepted as traditional sealing routine. Since his monograph was still the foremost exposition of the fur seals' peculiar life habits, an attack on him could endanger the main fabric of the American defense.

Had there been no vengeful Elliott to confute, Phelps could not have offset the damaging evidence of American negligence written by her servants, published in her own Federal printing office, where the full irresponsibility of the United States was plain to read. Too hampered by commercial pressure to make the bold—and belated—gesture of unselfish concern Elliott advocated and halt Pribilof sealing, the United States had come to court with soiled and shackled hands, unable to defend herself or her sea bears.

The fur seals' eccentric, amphibious habits had been a conundrum too complex for the neutral judges, who, Foster was satisfied, had striven to be fair, to solve. Baffled by descriptions of seal idiosyncrasies, they could neither conceive of them as private property nor realize the imperative need to revise ancient, established concepts of marine law to protect them. The trial had persuaded him there was no way to end pelagic killing until the United States demonstrated its disinterest in sealing profits and concern for the animals. If the herd were given time to recuperate—on land and sea—from its catastrophic losses, Foster pleaded, the regulations might yet afford it limited protection. Business-as-usual statesmanship stifled all pleas. International law decreed, for the next five years, at least, that at sea the fur seal was any man's target. The regulations went into effect.

Above the 35° north latitude, east of the 180° west longitude, from May to the end of July, pelagic sealing was forbidden in the Pacific Ocean and the Bering Sea; outlawed the year round within sixty miles of the Pribilof Islands. Only sailing schooners licensed by their own governments and flying special flags, could seal; only skilled marksmen be licensed as pelagic hunters. Each season captains must turn their logs over to their governments, a full record of the date and place of all killings, and the number and sex of each animal killed. Nets, firearms, and explosives were forbidden. Shotguns might be used only outside the Bering Sea. Indians, hunting in their canoes, could, provided their crafts were not transported to sealing grounds by a larger vessel, seal without license. Mutual agreement, at any time, could partially or wholly supersede the regulations.

Found guilty of unwarrantable interference with the rights of British subjects, the United States was ordered to stand trial for the seizure of ships and sealing equipment. Secretary of State Gresham persuaded Canada in 1894 to accept $425,000, instead of the $850,000 they asked, as full indemnity. Congress refused to provide that sum; the claim went to arbitration. A two-man commission held hearings in Victoria and San Francisco; a repentant Congress appropriated $473,151.26, nearly $50,000 more than Gresham's bargain, which was paid to Ambassador Pauncefote in June 1898.

The fur seal cared nothing for indemnities—only for its life which the Paris Award had put in jeopardy. Legal targets of shotguns on their routes between California and the Aleutian straits from February to May, of spear barbs anywhere in late summer sixty miles from the Pribilof Islands, the seals were doomed. Death's tempo quickened. A spear now ended three lives: the mother, the new fetal life within her, and her pup waiting in its rookery nursery. And beyond the longitudinal confine, the Asiatic fur seals lacked even the pretense of protection. The fur seal had seen Paris and come home to die.

16

The Plight of the Motherless

The trial was over. Summer came again. And the Pribilof fur seals, fleeing their law-protected piratical slayers, came homing to their islands. The bare rock ribs of the beaches jutted between the harems. As the summer passed, the song of the sealing beaches was pierced by the shrill pleas of hungry pups, waiting at the water's edge for absent mothers. Gradually their plaint weakened. Still no mothers hauled out of the surf to suckle them. Tiny throats were silenced. The starvelings lay quiet. Older seals trampled their shriveling bodies. Gulls and blue foxes prowled around the shrunken corpses and went away hungry. The waves reached inland, shifting the tiny dark bodies into windrows. The Seal Islands of the Bering, east and west, wore black mourning bands of infant dead on their sea rims. Then the autumn storms swept in to cleanse the land of man's crime. The surviving fur seals put to sea. Terror and greed settled down for a winter vacation. The beaches were quiet and clean.

In January 1895, Secretary of State Gresham summed up the partially known casualties of the first season of legalized pelagic killing: ". . . It would appear that there were landed in the United States and Victoria 121,430 skins, . . . the total pelagic catch, as shown by the London trade sales and careful estimates of skins transshipped in Japanese and Russian ports, amounts to about 142,000, a result unprecedented in the his-

tory of pelagic sealing." Although England refused to review
these damages, both nations began separate inquiries. Authorized to make a two-year study, a Commission, headed by Dr.
David Starr Jordan, reached St. Paul at the commencement of
the 1896 sealing season. Commending the project, Elliott took
exception to the selection of scientists connected with the Government and open (as he had been?) to suspicion of partisan-
ship. Although they were his personal friends, he spitefully
characterized them as "lightweights." Perhaps he foresaw his
title of fur seal expert would be lost to academic rivals.

Because uneven rookery surfaces defied correct estimation
of the space a fur seal occupied, the Commission repudiated
Elliott's law of uniform distribution and invented its own seal-
count system. For the orphans' sake, proof of the deadly effects
of the Paris regulations must be unassailable.

On the almost empty beaches the Commission's task was
simpler than in the days when Elliott and Maynard pioneered
as seal counters. It was possible to walk between the harems
and count the individual members of each family group. Jordan
selected the pups as the most reliable computation units. The
average number of infant seals in a family group was worked
out by an actual count on a small rookery. That average mul-
tiplied by the number of harems on a breeding beach—easily
tallied because each beachmaster towers so conspicuously above
his family, gave a fair approximation of its pup population.
Since multiple births are unknown, there had to be at least as
many cows as pups. Adding up the three groups, bulls, cows,
and pups, the total became a reasonably accurate rookery census. Nonbreeding seals defied the enumerators; their census remained a matter of surmise. Jordan's system was superseded
years later by one based on an annual geometric rate of increase. The 400,000 fur seals which the Commission computed
in 1897 contrasted tragically with Elliott's earlier census of
4,500,000, a figure Jordan dismissed as absurd. Despite its
commendable aspects, Jordan felt the tendency to consider

Elliott's system—and Elliott—infallible obliged him to expose its deficiencies. Perhaps he excoriated it the more happily because he believed gossip that Elliott was an English agent. Ill will between scientists added to the fur seal's problems.

As the summer drew to a close, the Commissioners turned from the census of the living to the sad labor of counting the motherless dead. They tallied 10,000 in a few days; hundreds more had died, but their bodies had rotted in rock crevices or been swept away by the waves.

Having disposed of Elliott's mathematics, Jordan explored his theory that overdriving during adolescence made bulls impotent. He branded it ridiculous. Basing his opinion only on drives he attended, he declared that the likelihood the few bachelors released from a roundup would suffer the exertion of repeated land marches, was slight. If breeding bulls were not vitiated by their frenzied harem activities, young males should be able to undergo frequent driving unscathed. Jordan did not note how many rejected seals, overcome by suffocation, died on their trip back to the sea, but today's seal managers follow them to save their skins at least if the seals die on the way.

The second season of lawful sea hunting was also fantastically lucrative. Over a hundred Canadian, American, and Japanese schooners brought at least 92,437 skins to market, but, in 1896, only 43,917 Pribilof skins and 24,191 from the Commander herd. Disappointed hunters, unwilling to admit the obvious reason, blamed stormy weather for the lower take. Weather reports for preceding years gave the lie to their excuse. Fewer bachelors were killed that year on land. Henceforth, seals and profits would decline together; each step downward marked by the windrows of dead pups on all Bering seal islands.

The British researchers of 1896, Professor D'Arcy Thompson and Mr. Macoun, predicted an approaching equilibrium as the lack of seals put pelagic hunters out of business, a mere figure of speech for diplomatic games, expostulated Dr. Jordan, as important to the fur seals' future salvation as the proverb,

"Death cures all ills." Death cured the orphaned pups' gnawing hunger. Was it the sole answer to the fur seals' desperate predicament?

Similar as were the reported observations of both nations' scientists, the British conclusions were strangely divorced from their findings. Political and patriotic motives guided scientific pens to repeat the stale assertion that land slaughter had decimated the herd. Great Britain was loath to review the regulations before the date set by the Paris court. American statesmen grew bitter. In May 1897, Secretary of State Sherman wrote his Ambassador in England, Mr. Hay: ". . . the British government has from the beginning and continuously failed to respect the real intent and spirit of the Tribunal or the obligations imposed by it. This is shown by the refusal to extend the regulations to the Asiatic waters; by the failure to put in operation the recommendation for a suspension of the killing of the seals for three, for two or even for one year; by the neglect to put the regulations in force until long after the first sealing season had been entered on; by the almost total evasion of the patrol duty; by the opposition to suitable measures for the enforcement of the prohibition against firearms; by the omission to enact legislations necessary to secure conviction of the guilty; and by the refusal to allow or provide for the inspection of skins in the interest of an honest observance of the regulations. . . . A course so persistently followed for the past three years has practically accomplished the commercial extinction of the fur seals and brought to naught the patient labors and well-meant conclusions of the Tribunal of Arbitrations . . ."

Poachers in restricted waters were shooting, not spearing, seals. A new American law ascribed guilt to sealers whose schooners carried firearms and bullet-marked furs. Canadians had to be seen shooting a seal before the British considered them guilty! During the 1894 closed season, the United States maintained a dozen armed vessels in the region; the British only one to supervise the larger Canadian fleet.

In the spring of 1897, while the Commission resumed its

studies in the north, the newly appointed "Seal Commissioners," John W. Foster and Charles S. Hamlin, organized a conference of all countries interested in the fur seals' future. Japan, not yet completely beggared of its fur-bearing sea animals, and Russia, directly ruling her seal islands after Hutchinson's Company left in 1893, immediately accepted, but not the English. Instead, Salisbury proposed a joint conference of the returning scientists in the fall—a conference devoid of plenary powers and closed to Russia and Japan, who had no scientists "in a position corresponding to that of the commissioners who have been carrying on their investigation upon the Pribilof Islands during the past two years." His intent to limit discussion to the Pribilof seals was clear. "Neither of the two countries in question [Russia and Japan] possesses any direct interest in the herd frequenting those islands."

Representatives of the United States, Japan, and Russia met in October 1897 and condemned pelagic sealing. They resolved to call an international conference to formulate effective sealing laws and agreed to prohibit their own citizens from seal hunting. Shamefully late in demanding of Americans the same restraint the United States asked of other nations, in December, Congress forbade United States citizens, aside from authorized lessees, to kill seals, and prohibited the importation of pelagic sealskins—"raw, dressed, dyed, or manufactured," thus excluding practically all but Pribilof sealskins from the American market. Salisbury saw "no useful purpose" in the resolutions of the October conference, since they contained "no provision for restricting the destruction of the seals on the Pribilof Islands by the American Company." Coerced by the political friends of the lessees, perhaps also genuinely fearful lest, even after the suspension of Pribilof sealing, Great Britain find further pretexts to continue pelagic hunting, American statesmen hesitated. They pleaded their lack of power to rescind or interrupt the lease, even if the lessees were compensated for their losses. It was known the latter would not be bought off easily. In 1892, Elliott had proposed, without success, to D. O. Mills, an officer of the North American Commercial Company, that the Company surrender its franchise in exchange for compensation secured by a "fair and just act of Congress." Indemnification for a broken lease would have been less costly than the attempts to convince Great Britain and Canadian sealers of American title to the Pribilof herd. In a few terse sentences British diplomats made the tripartite conference meaningless. Without British aid, no one of the three herds was safe.

At a reunion of the Bering Sea Commissioners in November 1897, hope for seal peace was rekindled. The English scientists had suffered a change of heart during their second summer on the seals' rapidly emptying beaches. Lined up with their American colleagues, they denounced pelagic hunting as the sole destroyer of seals and all kinds of pelagic sealing as incompatible with seal conservation. They even asserted that land killing had never contributed to the Pribilof herd's spoliation.

Confounded by their own experts, the Canadians still held out against the immediate *modus vivendi* John Foster requested. "There are difficulties in agreeing to that proposition which I fear will be found insuperable," Sir Wilfred Laurier informed him. "The fleet is preparing as usual; the prohibition of pelagic sealing for a year would practically destroy the business for several years, because the masters, the mates, and the crews, for the larger part belonging to other parts of Canada, would leave British Columbia. The sum which would likely be demanded as compensation is far beyond what it would be possible for us to induce Parliament to vote, even if we could recommend it. . . . I am in hope that you will not press for the immediate suspension of pelagic sealing." Another diplomatic defeat for the fur seals chalked up, the British "muddled through" successfully to the expiration date set by the Paris judges.

Then, a calm review of the effects of the Paris Award proved difficult because many critical problems, such as the Alaskan-Canadian border dispute, were also submitted to the Joint High Commission meeting in Quebec in 1898. Brief sessions in Washington alternated with long adjournments for many months. Canadian efforts to bargain fur seal safety for concessions advantageous to her in settling the other disputes failed. Then, indifferent to female casualties the pelagic sealers' logs revealed, undeterred by conclusions of English scientists, and unmoved by the statistics of motherless pups dead from starvation, Canada refused an American offer to buy her entire pelagic industry outright. She would hear no plea for a reform or renewal of the regulations. The Paris Award lapsed. The fur seals no longer had the pretense of legal protection. No nation dared interfere with hunters beyond the three-mile limit. Pelagic sealers—not the fur seals—had won a *zapusk*.

As long as a saleable seal traveled ocean lanes, no "equilibrium" discouraged its pursuit. American citizens, prohibited from sealing anywhere above 35° north latitude, or from buying skins taken in that area, could still outwit their Government profitably and Canadians get lucrative catches by investing in a Japanese flag and hiring low-paid Japanese seamen. In a season or two, Hakodate outrivaled Victoria as the pelagic hunters' home port.

America and her fur seals had lost. A natural resource monopolized by a single company had proved indefensible. The United States' scandalous neglect of its seals had sentenced them to marine firing squads. Nearly a million pelagic pelts had reached the market between 1868 and 1897. Other millions had died during the hunting. The motherless, born and unborn, that died because American statesmen held rigidly to conventional ideas of business as usual totaled an astronomical figure. They had all died because a small group of American businessmen, unable to forego a few seasons' profits, had fought, by fair means and foul, for their contractual right—and won.

To condone land killing, the Russian myth of the murderous males was revived: that while females perished at sea, a proportionate number of young males must be killed annually— that bachelors also were murdered at sea was not taken into account—to avoid the maturing of too many idle bulls. As puny and ridiculous as this resurrected rationalization must have sounded to others besides Elliott in 1897, it petrified into the unyielding defense of politicians, businessmen, and Government-employed scientists against his demand for a holiday from land killing.

Scientists gained no safety for the fur seal but their reports earned them sympathy, even in literary circles. Kipling's story of *The White Seal* carried the tragedy into the nursery. In many lands children hummed the mother seal's lullaby, wept over the seals' persecution, and rejoiced when the white seal led his kindred to an unknown island beyond the pelagic hunters' pursuit. Dr. Jordan's greatest achievement in the fur seals' behalf is his tender tale of *Matka*. Written deliberately to rouse pity for pelagic victims, this artless, poignant story of a mother seal revealed the horrors of seal hunting more vividly than the four huge volumes of fact his Commission compiled, and to a wider audience. That 122,000 infant seals died of hunger in 4 years was only a dry statistic. Human hearts ached as they read:

"At last came the sad year when the pirate ships that know no mercy found their way into the Icy Sea. It was then that we discovered Matka with a spearhead in her throat, dead on the shining sands of Zolotoi the golden. And Lakutha, that summer's baby, who had been so plump and playful, grew faint and thin until at last she starved and died."

Neither storytellers nor scientists won clemency for the doomed fur seal. North and south, east and west, the chase was on. Summer after summer the seal babies waited in vain for their mothers, writhed in convulsions on their birthrocks, and died by thousands. The promised "equilibrium" brought no peace to the dwindling survivors. Instead, fur pirates came boldly out of the sea to slay the seals on the forbidden soil of sovereign nations' territory.

17

Amnesty in the North Pacific

It was the sweep of schooners flying the Japanese flag from one migration route to another, from the Commander Islands to the Pribilofs and onto their shores, that drove most Canadian sealers out of business. Murderous gangs landed on St. George beaches far from the village. Protected by overhanging cliffs, they secretly killed their helpless prey and were gone. A broken club, skinned carcasses, or blood-splashed rocks betrayed their visits too late. Then, grown bolder or greedier, the pirates raided the more open expanses of St. Paul's beaches. Watchhouses were built on Pribilof rookeries; poorly armed lookouts were stationed on the beaches. Agents begged Washington for boats and weapons to drive off the raiders and for self-defense. The islanders were too few to guard all seal beaches simultaneously. Piratical schooners drifted impudently at anchor just outside the three-mile limit, launching small boats to kill swimming seals. Revenue cutters trailed them from rookery to rookery, lost them in the fog, and heard, without being able to interfere, the shots that killed the seals. The poachers had a keen sense for smelling out an unprotected beach. Frequent refueling of patrol vessels at Unalaska was necessary. No sooner had the cutter steamed beyond the horizon than the pirates sailed into view, usually flying Japanese colors. Few vessels belonged to Japanese citizens; the majority to owners of many nationalities —too many of them to Americans. The conflict between the

135

ill-matched forces of defenders and attackers went on until, in July 1906, St. Paul shores were stained with human blood.

The cutter was absent at Unalaska. The breeding season was at its peak. At least sixteen Japanese vessels ringed St. Paul, several anchored within the three-mile limit. Helplessly rookery sentinels listened to the poachers' gunfire. Occasionally through a rift in the heavy mists the alien boats were visible, close but beyond rifle range. Thirty-eight able-bodied men sharing twelve rifles prepared to defend the forty miles of coastline, knowing that if the well-armed crews of the poachers landed simultaneously they could offer no real defense.

Early on the morning of the sixteenth, three guards posted at Northeast Point spied a large schooner close to shore. One ran off to summon Agent Lembkey and reinforcements. Islanders hiding behind the natural ramparts of rocks saw a small boat, outfitted with mainsail and jib, put out from the vessel and pull directly toward the base of Hutchinson Hill. Six unsuspecting Japanese sailors climbed out of the boat and were immediately surrounded. One pleaded in broken English that they had come ashore only for fresh water. Sealing clubs, knives, and other gear, and a five-gallon cask full of fresh water gave the lie to his plea. Bound with greased cloth, the six oars rested in oarlocks so well padded that no sound could betray the boat's illegal presence. The raiders had come prepared to slay and steal the coveted furs. The prisoners were marched off along the twelve-mile road to the village.

During the remainder of the day, guards at every rookery waited alertly while guns barked eerily behind the curtain of fog. At intervals marauding schooners communicated by cannon signals with each other and their small butcher boats. Guards at Reef Point glimpsed a vessel close to shore. At Polovina Point, other watchers saw, for a few minutes, another sealer at work.

At 8 o'clock the next morning a second band of Japanese pirates in three small boats approached the western side of

Northeast Point under cover of the thick morning fog. The Aleut guards, Michael Kozloff and John Fratis, saw the lead boat at the shore line. Two sailors were busy with the sail. A third sat facing landward with a rifle in his hands. Kozloff and Fratis leaped from hiding and shouted, "Hands up!" Hastily the Japanese abandoned the sail and grabbed their oars; Kozloff fired three warning shots in the water close to the boat. The frantic sailors bent to their oars. The guards fired six more shots, aiming directly at the boat and its occupants. The Japanese slumped in their seats. The strong wind swept the boat back to the beach. Kozloff and Fratis ran to haul it up on the shingle. Inside lay two dead Japanese. The third man crouched in fright, nursing a wounded shoulder. The other boats had escaped back to the schooner when the alarm was given.

Offshore, rifle fire echoed through the fog at Zapadni in the afternoon. Suddenly the clouds of mist rolled away and two astonished guards gaped at three boats, holding eighteen or twenty sailors, a few yards from them. Frightened at the sight of such a large force, the guards shot wildly toward the boats, which swerved and headed for the open sea, unharmed by the hasty fusillade.

The captains of the schooners at Northeast Point were determined to get furs. All day long the staccato of rifle fire sounded. Frequently, the deadly bellow of the cannon signaled through the murky atmosphere, echoing and re-echoing among the rocks. Until eight in the evening, fog protected the marauders. Then guards spied a schooner anchored in dangerously shallow water three hundred yards off the Point's western shore. One raced to summon Lembkey and a squad of Aleuts. As they arrived, the fog bank was moving farther west. On the beach Japanese sailors were hastily embarking. Lembkey called to them to halt, but they leaped into their boats and rowed off madly. As bullets pattered over, around, and into the boats, all three turned shoreward to surrender. Then Lembkey realized his own force of fifteen Aleuts armed with six rifles was too small to insure capture of so many armed and desperate pirates. He permitted the first boat to land, then waved the others back to sea.

Gunfire from the schooner answered the Aleut attack on the landing party, but the bullets rained harmlessly into the surf. One dead Japanese sailor lay in the captured boat. Another toppled from one of the fleeing boats. His body floated from sight. Dead when he reached the schooner, a third was callously tossed overboard.

The five living prisoners, one wounded, huddled together while the guards inspected the rookery. The ravages were frightful: 183 seals had been victims. Skins of 120 were still in the surrendered boat. Sixty-three seals, either dead or wounded, lay scattered among the stones. Some, stunned by a blow on the head, had been skinned while still alive. These pitiful denuded animals staggered erect on mutilated flippers, scrambled first in one direction, then another. Their cries rose above the breakers in bewildered wails of pain until the horrified Aleut guards could end their anguish. Ruthlessly and savagely—and needlessly—the Japanese had beaten the threatening beachmasters across their protruding eyeballs until their eyes were smashed to bloody pulp. In the midst of the carnage intrepid, blinded males roared and plunged to meet unseen dangers and drive off invisible intruders. These, too, the weeping, cursing Aleut sealers mercifully killed. Only two of the murdered seals were males. The wanton slaughter of nursing mothers condemned 181 pups to die from slow starvation. Since no mark distinguished the orphans from more fortunate pups, the sealers could not save them from the long agony of death by starvation. Restraining their anger and hatred, the guards marched their prisoners back to join their fellows in the village lockup. Next day unwounded prisoners were led back to Northeast Point to dig a grave for their three dead companions. Near the scene of their crimes, where lupin and rosy *Pedicularis* wave gaily in summer, their bodies were hidden among the lichen-embroidered rocks. Much later their skulls were exhumed and for years lay in a dusty corner of the attic of the island physician's house. Whether thrown into the rubbish or carried off the island as gruesome souvenirs, their eventual disposition is unknown. Taken by cutter to Valdez, the prisoners received light sentences—three months' imprisonment—because they were only hired sailors obliged to carry out their officers' orders.

Human casualties were higher in the western Bering. Their Government had asked American consuls not to permit Japanese sailors to ship on American vessels. Yet in 1888, Copper Island guards, driving off raiders from the American sealer *Nemo,* killed three Japanese. In numerous affrays on Copper Island, a man or two on either side had lost his life. On one occasion poachers invaded the Commander Islands and kept a large defense force under siege in barracks for two weeks while they leisurely despoiled the rookeries.

The flotilla of Japanese sealing schooners which surrounded the island until the battle of Northeast Point taught them a degree of caution, was as great a threat to St. Paul's human inhabitants as to its animals. Had good fortune not attended Lembkey and the Aleuts, the pirates' depredations might not have ended with stripping furs from living seals. The Aleuts, dealing out death swiftly and painlessly with their clubs, earned their living killing seals, but their duties did not make them callous and brutal. The poachers could have slain the bulls as easily as blinding them. In fact, the pain only increased the bulls' outcries. Because the destruction of the fur seals meant the destruction of their livelihood, the Aleuts naturally hated all seal pirates. But the senseless cruelty of the Japanese poachers terrified the regular seal killers. The mutilation of the fur seals was an indelible horror the sealers could not forget. The memory of that July battle lived on in St. Paul history. Parents handed on their fear and hatred of the Japanese to their children.

The reign of terror continued for five years. Each season never less than twenty pirate ships besieged the Pribilofs, brazenly safe at anchor just beyond the three-mile limit. After that July raid more cutters were sent to guard the shores, but, under cover of fog, small boats still crossed the territorial line and bagged their furs. Many were arrested. Agent Lembkey, visiting the offshore table of Walrus Island, was interrupted by the arrival of three boatloads of men and hunting gear which he seized and turned over to a cutter. Another gang caught sight of this party on land and fled through convenient murk beyond gun range. Often Japanese sailors, who lost their schooners in the foggy seas, landed and were arrested, tried in Valdez or another Alaskan court, and, generally after a light jail sentence, were sent back to their homeland. Although the cutters could not effectively guard swimming seals, they did, after 1906, deter land raids.

"Black pups," Lampson and Sons advertised in their 1907 sales catalogue. The thrifty Japanese sealers turned in for sale the skins of unborn seals, ripped from their expiring mothers. George Clark, one of Dr. Jordan's assistant investigators, estimated a pup skin would bring about a sixpence in London. "The furriers will doubtless find a use for them. They may even appear as trimming on a lady's jacket. . . . What shall we say of a lady's jacket or muff made from the skins of unborn fur seal pups?"

Examining the Pribilof herd after an absence of thirteen years, Clark grieved that Dr. Jordan's experiments had been abandoned without proper trial. If all females were branded, their disfigured pelts would not be saleable. Then, if all rejected and reserved bachelors were marooned in an almost land-locked bay for the duration of each summer, the poachers would be forced out of business. Branded fur seals might have earned the status of straying branded cattle, property a finder was obliged to return to its owner. As Clark stood once more on a Pribilof rookery in 1909, he wrote sadly in his field notes: "I have again reviewed this bitter phenomenon of starving pups."

Why, after nearly a half century of bitter wrangling and successive diplomatic crises veering dangerously toward open warfare, all opposition to fur seal protection at sea abruptly collapsed is not easy to account for. No hint of the immediate incentive occurs in official documents. That only 130,000 fur seals survived on the Pribilof Islands—even fewer on the Asiatic seal beaches—was not the compelling factor. Poachers could have carried on profitably for a few more seasons. It was not because Japan had captured most of the pelagic trade. The Canadians—like American citizens—could and did seal under the Japanese flag. Indemnity in exchange for restraining their citizens from sealing was not the major lever to move the pelagic nations to acquiesce. It can only be that the fur seals' few friends, crusading tirelessly, had awakened in all lands so deep a public interest and sympathy for the unfortunate survivors that Great Britain, at least, felt morally obliged to concur in plans to save the Bering Sea fur seals from extinction. At any rate, all governments seemed suddenly weary of the conflict and hastened to accept one more American invitation to outlaw open-water sealing.

The attitudes of Japan and Russia had been so vacillatory as to be enigmatic. Russia and Great Britain signed, in 1895, a sealing truce modeled after the Paris regulations, except that the prohibited zone extended only thirty miles from Russia's seal islands. Yet she never protested England's failure to patrol the area and halt her nationals' flagrant violations of that treaty. She had paid damages which Great Britain demanded for seizures of Canadian vessels caught in the act of violating the rules —even those apprehended within the three-mile limit—without protest.

Sheltering most of the pelagic fleet after 1898, Japan made no official complaint when her citizens were punished by Russian or American courts, not even when they were killed raiding foreign seal rookeries. Only Great Britain, with amazing statecraft, had actively protected her seal killers.

In 1911 the North Pacific Sealing Convention was ratified by the four powers. Their nationals were forbidden to kill seals in the Pacific and the Bering above 30° north latitude. Entitled to trial in their own country, lawbreakers could be arrested by any one of the signatories. There was little demand for seal-skins outside of the United States, Great Britain, and Canada. So refusal to import sealskins unless clearly identified as taken on land destroyed the market for pelagic skins, and left other countries without an incentive to begin ocean sealing. The right of aborigines to hunt in a canoe and spear seals was upheld. Japan and Canada were each assigned 15 per cent of the annual Pribilof catch, payable either in pelts or cash. Russia pledged a similar proportion of her sealskins to both nations. In return, Japan was to remit 10 per cent of her catch to each of her three co-signers. Minimum killing quotas were defined; provision made for immediate cash compensation in the event of suspending land killings. Such advances were, in the case of the United States, recoverable at the rate of 4 per cent of the yearly take when the killings were resumed. The terms, manda-tory for 15 years were, if unopposed, to have permanent status. However, any nation could, during the fifteenth year or at any subsequent date, submit a notice of resignation, to take effect a year later.

In the United States, the Treaty indirectly aroused a new domestic sealing controversy because, coincidentally, Congress proposed to give the exhausted Pribilof herd a holiday on land at last. It meant, of course, an immediate expenditure of at least $200,000 against a delayed future sealing income. To some Americans a recess seemed a confession that land sealing had been injurious to seal life. Even President Taft, reversing opin-ions he had expressed to Congress the preceding year, argued that the United States was losing an opportunity to demonstrate absolutely the innocuous nature of supervised land slaughter. But the sentiment in Congress, spurred by Henry Elliott, began to catch up with the spirit of international compassion. All northern fur seals had won amnesty at sea. The Pribilof seals had still to win an armistice on their Alaskan islands.

18

The Fur Seal
Goes to Congress

The fur seal was long in winning redress from international councils; longer in settling its domestic affairs. Petitioning Congress for protective management, its case was complicated by partisan politics, bureaucratic ignorance and prejudice, and the lobbying of wolfish commercial interests. The lessees of their islands had friends and stockholders in Congress. The fur seals had few friends and but one indefatigable lobbyist, Henry Wood Elliott. Until those barren rocks he had seen in 1890 teemed as abundantly with fur seal life as in 1872, Elliott's conscience bound him to the fur seals' service.

He set to work to prove that the lessees, unable to fill their quota, were killing young seals and deliberately leaving excess blubber on their skins so that, by weight, they appeared to be pelts of legal-sized animals. Seal managers had no idea how much a fur seal pelt of any age should weigh or whether a salted skin weighed more or less than an unsalted one. Confronted with Elliott's exact tables, embarrassed fur seal caretakers writhed in the witness chair, unable to answer the insufferable inquisitioner prating of weights and measurements, spouting his eternal, unanswerable "facts." From 1903 to 1905 it seemed the fur seals might soon win their case.

Headed by Senator Dillingham, a senatorial committee visited the Pribilof seals in 1903 and saw, on the killing field, three females clubbed to death—an inevitable accident, protested Agent Lembkey, because the August 4th drive, arranged for the Senators, was out of season. Sooner or later, agents adopted Elliott's theories, put them into practice quietly or borrowed them in self-defense without acknowledging their author. So Lembkey shamelessly fell back on the premise which Goff and Elliott had fathered, that killing should end before harem boundaries became fluid, soon after mid-July, which for years had been so savagely combated by local Pribilof custodians, his predecessors.

Convinced, nevertheless, that Elliott's charges were correct, the indignant Senators reported to Congress that the 200,000 Pribilof survivors deserved a 5-year holiday. But Dillingham's bill to save the fur seal was neatly maneuvered from his Committee by the lessees' more adroit senatorial friends to the Committee on Foreign Relations, where it was tabled—for eternity.

After the defeat of the Dillingham bill and the rupture of the latest treaty discussions with England due to Secretary Hay's death, and because, in 1906, higher prices induced more Canadians to go sealing, Elliott felt that perfidy, greed, and terror on land and sea were too strong for one man to combat. Abandoned by old friends, slandered by his enemies as insane, a squaw man, and a traitorous Canadian agent, Elliott in 1907 sent Professor William T. Hornaday, Director of the New York Zoo, a simple appeal: "Do something to save the fur seals." At the Boston meeting of the International Zoological Congress that summer Hornaday's resolution condemning pelagic sealing and calling for international protection for the fur seals was defeated in committee by the elderly Russian delegate who protested he lacked power to meddle in foreign affairs.

Although public controversy whether 130,000 or 30,000 Pribilof seals still lived grew fiercer, nothing decisive happened during the next two years. Even the Canadian Toronto *Globe* editorialized: "If this fur seal business has ever been equalled

(*Above*) Around the Branding Table—Branding Operations on St. Paul

(*Below*) A Bachelor Roundup for Branding Experiment

St. Paul Aleuts Ready for a Sunday Outing

for organized deception and hidden political influence, the world has never been enlightened by the disclosure."

In 1909 Hornaday "shouldered the Thankless Task," as he wrote later, to find out whether private individuals could defy entrenched greed and, against frightful odds, save the fur seal. Calling his request "brutal," he asked Elliott to remain in the background preparing evidence and arguments for him to present in public. Elliott consented, confident he had an ally not easily to be impugned by the lessees' friends. Both were to learn that no one who advocated a recess from seal killing could escape calumny.

Backed by such influential supporters as the Camp Fire Club of America, Hornaday rallied Senator Joseph M. Dixon, Chairman of the National Resources Committee, to the fur seals' cause. A Camp Fire Club appeal to the general public, entitled "The Loss of the Fur Seal Industry," appeared in twenty-five newspapers in December 1909. Hornaday predicted the campaign would be a "love feast." Years later he could laugh at his naïveté when he ventured into the "Hornet Nest" of Washington, yet his initial success confirmed his prediction. At the first hearing before Dixon's Committee, its eleven members listened for nearly two hours to Hornaday's presentation of the fur seals' case, as it had been briefed by Elliott, and unanimously resolved to ask the Department of Commerce and Labor, the fur seals' new guardians, to issue no sealing franchise when the current one expired in April, but to wait enactment of new sealing legislation. A bill was drawn up which incorporated abolition of the leasing system; conclusion of a treaty between England, Japan, and Russia to end pelagic sealing on a percentage compensation basis; and immediate suspension of land killing for a five- to ten-year period. Dixon's colleagues approved the measure, and Dixon introduced it in the Senate.

Elliott warned Hornaday that, when the bill was presented, a member of the Committee on Foreign Relations would rise to ask its referral to his committee, to be tabled forever as the

Dillingham bill had been. Skeptically, Hornaday passed the warning on to an equally skeptical Dixon. But, as predicted, the Senator whom Elliott had named argued plausibly that, because the State Department was on the verge of concluding a treaty with Japan and England, the bill belonged to his committee. (Hornaday investigated—the State Department was not even on the threshold of serious negotiations.) To save his bill from being kidnaped, Senator Dixon promptly tabled it. Two months later, when his colleague of the Foreign Relations Committee was absent, Dixon recalled his resolution, and the Senate referred it back to his own committee.

Dixon's rescue of his resolution upset the plans of the Commerce and Labor Department. Secretary Nagel had been preparing to accept bids for sealing rights despite the unanimous joint recommendations of the Advisory Board of the Fur Seal Service of which Dr. Jordan was a member and the Fur Seal Board of his own Bureau of Fisheries, submitted to him the previous November. They suggested many excellent reforms: only Government agents should determine annual quotas and manage sealing; the lessee should "be restricted to the receiving, curing, and shipping of the skins taken," and—appeasement to Elliott?—skins should weigh at least five pounds. Experience had brought most former scientist opponents much closer to Elliott's point of view but, unable to forget past feuds, they did not join forces to help the fur seals. Official advisers did no more than recommend.

To press home those recommendations, one had to be an Elliott. A peculiar pessimistic stagnation existed in the Bureau of Fisheries, possibly due to nagging obligations to return political favors. Even staff naturalists had trouble thinking of fur seal conservation problems as distinct from market ones. Only a desire to crush and silence Elliott ever bestirred that official lethargy.

At the Dixon Committee hearings, Secretary Nagel and Agent Lembkey evinced the usual bureaucratic despondency, introducing the fur seal's scapegoat, the Pribilof Aleuts whose livelihood depended on the continuance of seal killing. Dixon promised that Congress would provide an annual subsidy of $50,000 during a holiday and permit the Aleuts to kill 2,500 seals a year for fresh meat. President Taft, influenced by Dr. Hornaday and the Camp Fire Club, instructed Congress to hasten domestic conservation of the fur seal.

Seemingly Secretary Nagel capitulated to public and political demands and presented a bill he called more adequate than the Dixon measure, making Pribilof sealing a function of his Department. It contained no provision for a seal holiday, but Hornaday accepted, as a gentleman's agreement, Nagel's vague intimation that for some years fur seals would be killed only for the Aleuts' food. Hornaday, the Camp Fire Club, Congress, and the general public thought the seals' domestic troubles were over when the bill became law, April 21, 1910. For nine days the fur seals' friends rejoiced. Nine days! On May 1st, the Commissioner of Fisheries, Mr. Bowers, informed Seattle reporters that fur seals would be killed for commercial purposes because they should be killed. The myth that excess males would destroy the herd was exhumed to excuse official sealing philosophy. A "gentleman's agreement" meant nothing to commercial-minded sealing bureaucrats.

An embittered Hornaday took Secretary Nagel to task, asking; ". . . Did the President, or did Senator Dixon's committee, or the United States Senate intend for one moment that you should go right on in the bloody killing business without a halt? No! A thousand times, no, and you know it! Was it not partly for the purpose of cleaning our hands of fur seal blood and clearing the road for treaties by the State Department that the new law was driven through Congress? You now propose to nullify the whole act, and set up Lembkey in the killing business in place of the North American Commercial Co. When you and I were before the Senate Committee, I saw clearly what was in Lembkey's mind, and at last I suspected what was in yours. It was then that I demanded of you a positive assurance regarding your intentions, some proof that you were giving the committee a square deal. And what did you reply? You were careful to give no assurance whatever. You merely shifted uneasily in your chair and said, 'I would like to have the right to kill seals, for I think it would be a good thing to hold it as a club over the heads of the pelagic sealers,' or words to that effect. Now, what is it that you are really going to do? You propose to use the bloody club on the seals themselves forthwith; and you propose to pay good Government money for a lot of old junk with which to carry on the seal-slaughtering business."

Despite the public outcry, the Bureau of Fisheries killed 12,920 of the 130,000 remaining fur seals—bachelors too young for commercial killing, according to Elliott's standards of weights and measurements. As enraged and baffled as Elliott had been in his loneliest moments, Hornaday summoned the old warrior from backstage. "One of my answers to the seal killers," he wrote decades later, "was Henry Wood Elliott." Fight as you see fit was Hornaday's only advice.

Immediately, Elliott preferred charges of misconduct against the Department of Commerce and Labor. Hearings opened before the House Committee on Expenditures in the Department of Commerce and Labor, headed by Representative Rothermel of Pennsylvania, May 21, 1911, and dragged on for almost three years—until March 4, 1914. The fur seals' advocate briefed their complaints and crossquestioned their legal guardians. Only Secretary Nagel escaped the merciless probing questions of prosecutor Elliott.

As usual his charges of abuse and neglect inspired hasty investigations. Inquiries which should have been the reasonable routine duties of naturalist-custodians of the seals were undertaken merely to disprove his contentions. Pup counting had to be reviewed, sealskins had to be weighed and measured—before salting and after. George Clark, Secretary of Stanford University, grilled on his 1909 studies, insisted live pups could be counted without risk of being injured in the stampedes caused by the intruding census takers, because they paraded before the estimators as calmly as sheep going through a gate. Outraged by the simile, it became a scathing barb in Elliott's diatribes against fur seal mistreatment. The elevated runways, erected later over the rookeries to eliminate all risk of disturbing breeding seals, are a monument to Elliott's correct but unacknowledged judgment.

The arguments over salted skins were futile because the disputants could compare only those treated by different methods at different times. Elliott's serious charge of "loading"—leaving excess blubber to make the skins appear to be those of older animals—was excused, if not explained away, by Lembkey as the work of young, inexperienced sealers who feared to remove too much fat lest they cut the skins.

In 1913, commissioned by the House Committee to inspect the seals, Elliott revisited St. Paul Island. In vain Agent Lembkey assigned men to accompany Elliott. The old man rose too early in the morning, tramping about muttering, according to one witness, "Like sheep through a gate!" While Elliott was still gathering data, a telegram informed Lembkey that Elliott and the fur seals had won. The Republican majority on the committee had cast their votes for a five-year holiday and were referring charges against Fisheries officials and the North American Commercial Company to the Attorney General, with a demand for prompt action. The Democrats, in the minority, opposed both resolutions. Partisan politics, for once, sided with the persecuted fur seal.

There are stories still current on the Pribilofs of that last visit of the "man with the pencil." One noon Elliott came into the dining room while Agent Lembkey was at lunch and flung a fat, bloody pelt on the table as proof of careless flensing. Lembkey clapped a hand to his mouth and dashed for the door. "He couldn't eat for a week," related the Aleut who had witnessed the scene in his boyhood.

Elliott's attitude toward the sealers had mellowed since his first visits to their islands. Reminding them that he had married a local girl and objected to their being cheated, he urged them to fight for their rights—and the seals'. His incendiary language did not kindle a people who had learned from bitter experience that while God was high and the Czar far, Washington was even farther. For too many years the Aleuts had feared that fur seal extinction would force them to abandon their home islands or starve. So, when the fur seals won their holiday, and they were authorized to be their sole legal killers, a prerogative assuring them a measure of immediate economic security and protecting their Pribilof residence rights, the islanders welcomed governmental recognition of their ancient ties with the seals which would later prove to be galling bonds.

By 1914, then, it seemed that the last battle of the fur seal at home or abroad had been won. Henceforth and forever the fur seals were safe on land and sea. The champion, over sixty years old, welcomed retirement to his real estate business and a tranquil old age in his Cleveland "vineyard."

While Rothermel prodded Attorney General McReynolds to prosecute the North American Commercial Company for the alleged illegal killing of 128,000 yearling males, thereby defrauding the Government of millions of dollars, a trio of researchers, sent north by Secretary Nagel to time the arrival of yearling seals, reported back at the summer's end that no yearlings returned to their birthplace before August. Consequently, even in late July roundups none could be encircled and killed. If their observations were exact, Elliott's contention that the lessees had killed yearlings was baseless; Jordan's reports that one-year-old males came in mid-July, the yearling females later, and Clark's field note jottings that he had seen yearlings come ashore in July, were delusions; Agent Lembkey's admissions that yearlings were caught up in seal drives were erroneous; and the Committee's charges were founded on false premises. If the Attorney General prosecuted, the ex-lessees' defense was ready, gratuitously provided by a Government agency, and the officials of that Bureau were cleared of all suspicion of negligence. Only years later would it be dispassionately decided that the only safeguard against killing yearlings and females—as Goff stated in 1890—was to stop seal drives about July 20.

The North American Commercial Company was never brought to trial; its profits, estimated as about $5,000,000, while the Government's loss during their tenure was nearly $1,500,000, were undisturbed. The Treasury was never indemnified for its losses. Secretary of Commerce Redfield notified McReynold's successor, Attorney General Gregory, that, since recent findings made it certain there had been no small seals on the Pribilofs during the regular sealing seasons, he could not support the prosecution. Without that aid, Mr. Gregory felt he had no case. Elliott's personal appeal for Secretary Redfield's co-operation was rejected. Official arguments that past embarrassments were better forgotten prevailed. The Rothermel report gathered dust in the files. The death of 128,000 young seals became an unsolved mystery.

Pribilof sealing was resumed in 1917. Only Government managers supervised the slaughter. New safeguards—annual seal counts, obligatory records and other procedures—insured the herd against future damage. Their champion should have been in his Cleveland vineyard, happily attending to personal business matters.

19

The Champion's Last Crusade

The alarm that drew the old battler from his corner, bristling and fighting mad, was Secretary Redfield's announcement during a public speech in Cleveland, the champion's home territory, in 1916, that the St. Louis furrier, Funsten Brothers, had been engaged to process the furs and sell them for the Department. Even while the ink was drying on legislation which prohibited private monopoly of sealing, the fatal silver fleece had inspired enterprising minds to devise a novel and unprecedented exclusive claim to fur seal benefits. Like Hutchinson, Philip Fouke, guiding spirit of Funsten Brothers, had been early and successful; he was proud of his foresight.

"I came to Washington first in 1910 when Secretary Nagel was in office," Fouke informed a Senate Commerce Committee meeting. Finding Fisheries officials sympathetic to his plan to transfer the fur seal industry from London to the United States and, naturally, to his own city and his own factory, he made ready to process the skins as soon as the seal holiday ended. It had not been easy. In London, Fouke found Rice and Brothers, a leading fur seal dresser, unwilling to sell their secret dye formula. No price was sufficient compensation to risk damaging their own business. So he persuaded two of their furriers to come to the United States as his employees. Their dye formula lost without recompense, Rice and Brothers sued the United States Government and Funsten Brothers, and won damages. Forbidden by court to utilize the Rice formula, Fouke submitted one which the Bureau of Standards approved. Funsten Brothers was free, then, to handle Pribilof sealskins. The loss of duty formerly collected on nearly three quarters of London's dyed skins, which had been shipped to America to be made into garments, represented a sizable annual sum. The nation's income from the people's fur seals would be reduced to the amount left from the sales after Funsten Brothers' charges for processing skins and their auction commission were deducted.

Despite its advantages, Funsten Brothers was not financially successful. Within a few years Philip Fouke organized a new firm, the Fouke Fur Company, in St. Louis also, but incorporated under the laws of the State of Delaware. In 1921 Secretary of Commerce Alexander awarded the new company a ten-year contract to handle sealskins.

Shocked and frightened, Elliott watched the development of the new Government-approved sealskin monopoly. Aware of the insidious effect visions of fur seal profits exercised, a contract with a private firm for any purpose was a warning that sealing management might one day revert wholly to private industry. No guarantee existed that a future Congress, ignorant of the fur seals' past sufferings, would not rescind the protective legislation.

Elliott had always held that the fur seals as national property should contribute to national income. He had been satisfied with the rent and tariff proceeds which the first franchise yielded, but he no longer trusted a private company, especially one with monopolistic privileges, to guard the nation's resources. Treasury receipts from judicious, Government-supervised sealing would, he felt, be drastically whittled down by paying agents to dress, dye, and market the skins. "The seal industry is destroyed now, so far as the public Treasury is concerned," he fumed.

Amassing his statistics, he advanced once more on Washington. He initiated hearing after hearing on resolutions proposing that the Commerce Department market raw, salted sealskins without the aid of a middleman, exhibiting uncontestable proof that returns from sales of salted skins were more lucrative to the national Treasury. With amazing rapidity, Government circles revolved to present a new unanimity. Officials became conservationists disinterested in profits. Any discussion of sealing income was incompatible with fur seal preservation. "After all," stated the Secretary of Commerce, Herbert Hoover, "the question of financial return from the herd is quite secondary to its conservation." Exactly how the fur seals were to suffer from insuring that no unnecessary portion of the sales price be diverted from the Treasury into the tills of a private firm remains unexplained in all official statements.

Into the testimony, Elliott introduced some of his famous "deadly parallels." Side by side he listed the proceeds of raw skin sales and subsequent agent-handled auctions. For 12,920 salted skins taken in 1910 and sold in London by the Department of Commerce, the Treasury had received a net profit of $280,000; for 12,002 pelts the next year, $270,194. But two sales of dressed skins, held by the Fouke Fur Company, in October 1922 and May 1923, a total of 35,313 pelts, netted the United States only $260,000 after the expenses were deducted from the gross sales figure of $1,106,000. For three times the number of skins!

He demanded all skins be measured on the islands at killing time to assure that none shorter than 37½ inches be taken. He argued that the contractor who paid a flat rate for finishing skins would be indifferent to the slaughter of young fur seals, particularly because small skins were easier to handle. If skins measured in St. Louis were too small, it was too late to reprimand careless sealers. Secretary Hoover objected that skin measuring on the islands would entail too much labor. As with most of Elliott's proposals, this practice was adopted later. Dead seals are measured today on Pribilof killing fields before they are skinned.

An epidemic of forgetfulness plagued officeholder witnesses. Under Secretary of Commerce Huston could not recall the date of the original Funsten contract, was extremely unsure of Philip Fouke's previous connection with Funsten Brothers, and thought it quite probable that Funsten Brothers had won the Rice and Brother's suit for damages. On one subject he and other Fisheries' officials were enthusiastically voluble. The public, they argued, preferred to pay higher prices for superior, standard-graded furs furnished by a monopoly than to buy at lower prices the probably irregular and imperfectly dressed furs processed by small, independent furriers. Only the Fouke Fur Company, with its imported skilled furriers, its secret dye formula approved by the Bureau of Standards, and its especially equipped factory, could turn out standardized, well-dyed furs. Other American furriers knew nothing about dyeing sealskins.

Marshaling his facts methodically, Elliott related the history of fur seal dyeing, successfully undertaken in Albany, New York, as early as 1829. More than two dozen furriers had dressed sealskins during the 19th century. The most efficient machine for removing guard hairs had been designed in America. Not until American furriers had been lured to England to teach their craft to English fur workers had London become the center of the fur seal industry. One American who became a British subject for that purpose in 1842 had been C. M. Lampson, founder of the company that handled Hutchinson's sealskins and had so earnestly entreated the British to halt pelagic sealing. (Lampson had been made a baronet by Queen Victoria for his support of the Atlantic Cable project. The fur seal had directly or indirectly helped finance a variety of private and public projects.) Not all American sealskin dressers, however, had gone abroad. Treadwell and Company had won international repute at the Philadelphia Centennial exposition in 1876 for their rich chestnut sealskin dye. Elliott argued that a monopoly, unchallenged by no competitor perfecting finer dressed furs, might be content indefinitely with any kind of finish that sold. Given an opportunity, American furriers would not only dress sealskins competently but vie with each other to improve the furs.

To contradict his tiresome facts, officials parading year after year to the witness box, intoned their monotonous litany of the unique advantages of Fouke's methods, the need to preserve the seals and keep the seal industry in American hands. Each year Elliott's bill failed to pass. Like Hutchinson, Fouke Fur Company had political friends. As a keen entrepreneur, Fouke missed no opportunity to win political and public favor; the presentation of a sealskin coat to Mrs. Warren G. Harding was publicized as important news. Elliott had only his "facts," and his perseverance. No dramatic issues drew gore from journalists' pens as in the days of the pelagic sealing controversy, and the newspapers deemed the public weary of fur seal problems. Verbal fireworks sputtered frequently, but fizzed to nothingness in the Congressional chambers. Behind the old champion, supporters repugnant to him twisted his efforts to conserve a national resource so that it yielded the maximum benefit to the owner of its breeding stones, into ugly anti-Semitic propaganda.

The stench of anti-Semitism had clung to fur seal pelts since 1867. Critics of the mad scramble to be first at Sitka had bruited sly tittle-tattle about the many California Jewish merchants among the greedy bargain hunters and, overlooking Hutchinson, had insinuated the successful buyers were Jews. That some of Hutchinson's associates in the Alaska Commercial Company were Jews was often mentioned by his business rivals to disparage him. Jewish stockholders and officials of the North American Commercial Company had been blamed for that firm's alleged sharp practices. Whenever possible during national and international fur seal disputes, the animals' foes had slyly inserted the adjective "Jewish" to defame their opponents. Elliott's attacks against the Fouke Fur Company were acclaimed by organized anti-Semitic groups as a challenge to the Jewish octopus which was strangling American business. Ordinary commercial transactions between the Fouke Fur Company and foreign firms, particularly Eitington Schild Co., were attacked as machinations of "international Jewry." Henry Ford's *Dear-*

born Independent crudely stated: "The Jews are not going to lose their grip on the fur industry."

The desire for profit from the silver fleece was limited by no national boundaries; the urge to exploit the fur seal restricted to no one religious community. Protestant, Catholic, Jew, Greek Orthodox, and Shintoist had hunted the fur seals. Americans, British, Russians, Japanese, Europeans—men from practically all nations—had been lured by the fur seals' velvet fleece to scheme for its possession. Eternally begetting cupidity and deceit, the fur seal had the misfortune to be infamously manipulated by anti-Semites.

To defend his bill introduced by Senator Wheeler, Elliott came once more before the Senate's Commerce Committee in 1926. His eightieth birthday had passed. Failing health and dimming eyesight had forced him to give up the real estate business which sustained him during his long crusade. His testimony showed no signs of impaired health or of failing and confused memory, but his words were futile. Submitting written arguments against his resolution, Department of Commerce functionaries boycotted the hearings, confident the bill would die, as usual, in the committee room. Soon Elliott, too, would die. Then, busy officials would no longer be harassed by the troublemaker's public criticism. Dr. Townsend, a scientist who had often testified in behalf of Government sealing policy, had predicted: "I see no end to agitation on the subject of the fur seals as long as he is living, and the fact that he has been repeatedly discredited seems to make no difference."

Elliott opened his statement with the phrase he had so often pronounced within Congressional chambers: "The accident of my life made me the first . . ." Chance arranged that meeting between the callow, romantic scientist and the fur seals, but it was no accident that his life had been spent in their service. New ranks of opponents had formed against him with every change of national administration to carry on the feud like a sacred inheritance. His stubborn fight for fur seal conservation was belittled by successive phalanxes of adversaries as proof of his mental derangement. Unfaltering surety that his cause was just, his facts incontrovertible, kept the old champion consecrated to the service of his fur seals and his country. The hearing dragged on dully and adjourned; the bill a scrap of useless paper. The old man had done his best, but he had not won a larger share of sealing proceeds for his countrymen.

To be near his children, Elliott was living in Seattle in 1930, sketching Mount Rainier's various moods. At eighty-four he was still alert, an interested observer of public affairs. His correspondence with key men in government, with conservationists and scientists, was voluminous. A few months before he died, he wrote his brother-in-law in California: "I only did what any right-minded citizen would have done." When, after a week's illness, Elliott died, no "right-minded" citizen succeeded him as the fur seals' defender. No posthumous honors have been paid him; the seals he saved, but his reputation, tarnished by the slanders of powerful foes, has still to be rescued. His deeds are permanently recorded in dozens of volumes of Congressional hearings. Few Americans will chance to open even one to chuckle at his barbed rejoinders, his searing caustic epithets, or be impressed by his masterly, insistent repetition of embarrassing facts and statistics. No one following his course through volume after volume of these records will fail to be convinced that had there been no Elliott, the fur seal of the North Pacific might today be an aquatic wraith, companion to its vanished southern relative and to Steller's sea cow.

Mourning the friends he had lost during the fur seal disputes, Professor Hornaday was proud that at least one man—Henry Wood Elliott—called him friend. Published soon after his death, these words are the tribute Elliott would most have cherished. Sadly Hornaday concluded: "By the year 2000, Mr. Elliott's great-great-grandchildren may receive for him the thanks of Congress! But I doubt it."

20

The Self-Supporting Fur Seal

Ransomed from their sea assassins by the treaty of 1911, the North Pacific fur seals have survived two world wars, a revolution, a brief revival of pelagic hunting and other vicissitudes. They breed no more on Kuril Island's fog-swathed rocks though passers-by pull ashore to rest, but both Asiatic herds, under Soviet tutelage, convalesce steadily from the bloodletting of the latest sea hunting. Only the Pribilof dynasty is restored and hale. A recent treaty promises seal peace at sea and between nations. If no disruption of the tried and proved methods of the last four decades of sealing occur, the northern herds will thrive, defray the costs of their safe-conduct warrants and profit landlord nations who own their birthplaces. That fur seal peace remain unbroken and its silver fleece provoke no more dissension, hard-won historical lessons must never be forgotten.

Only a nation can defend the fur seals once they leave their natal beaches. The battles to insure the perpetuation of the species demonstrated for all time that, because of its polygamous nature and its dual terrestrial and seagoing life pattern, the fur seal is a troublesome asset that only a nation can manage wisely; its breeding island a vulnerable outpost only a nation can guard from sea raiders. Residents of Alaska, dreaming of fat revenue from the Pribilof seal bank to develop their new state rapidly, may contend the islands should be state adminis-

tered. Unless the history of fur sealing, the international con-
flicts the seal occasioned—barely resolved in time to rescue the
species from extinction—are kept in mind, arguments for state
control will sound plausible. As Pribilof residents, American
sealers are entitled to the benefits and responsibilities of citizens
of the forty-ninth state, but Pribilof seals must remain the property of the citizens of all fifty states, *or there will be no fur seals.*

Because the American herd which breeds on the two larger of
the Pribilof Islands, St. George and St. Paul, and a crescent-
shaped islet, Sea Lion Rock, close to the latter, comprises eighty
per cent of the world's fur seals (The other twenty per cent in-
clude the Commander and Robben Island herds and the widely
separated colonies of survivor descendants of former mighty
Antarctic seal populations.), Americans bear the heaviest bur-
den of all seal island owners. Not only must they protect their
own American-born animals wherever they wander along foreign coasts or in midocean, and encourage their propagation—
resisting temptation to overexploit their furred treasure trove
for profit at the expense of the herd's well-being, but they must
be champions of and spokesmen for all fur seals. Their handling
of seals and seal furs must be so scrupulously impeccable that
it be a model all seal island proprietors, north and south of
the equator, respect and imitate; must be so exemplary no envious detractor can ever again prevent seal conservation on the
grounds, once so fatal, that their guardians' hands are blood-
stained, their abuse of seal life a scandal. The gravity and
global scope of American responsibility were not suspected
when the Bureau of Fisheries became administrator of the
Pribilof Islands in 1909. Sparked first by Elliott's goading,
prodded by increasing public criticism, Bureau officials resisted
and fumbled—and erred frequently, but, as years passed, they
began to understand that the United States has a moral obliga-
tion to conserve the eccentric amphibious mammal, that the
animal possesses a higher worth than its prevailing market
price, and that, treated well, it can pay its own way. This wak-
ening philosophy of conservation first, fur profits second, bol-

stered by the conviction that public opinion must be satisfied, gradually dominated American sealing policies.

The Fish and Wildlife Service of the Department of Interior, formed by a merger of the Bureau of Fisheries in 1936 with the Biological Survey, manages the fur seals, the sealskin industry and the seals' islands, and is now the resident sealers' employer.

Between the signatories of the Sealing Convention there was no serious bickering over the sea bears for decades. Only Japan desired to revise the Convention in 1926 but, when other international complications prevented calling all interested countries together to hear her criticisms, made no further complaint. No other nation commenced pelagic sealing. Hunted only by American Indians, Ainus, and other littoral peoples along their migratory sea tracks, guarded on land, accompanied on migration by signatories' patrol vessels, the northern seals recuperated from pelagic massacre and yielded larger crops of furs each season. Yearly the United States paid Canada and Japan their shares of the sale proceeds on Alaskan pelts in cash until, in 1933, the Canadians requested their share in raw skins. Japan shipped annually to her consignees a hundred or more Robben Island furs. After 1935, her herd having increased, she doubled the number. Neglected during World War I and for years after the overthrow of the Czar, the Commander seals were delayed in making a comeback. It was not until about 1922 that scientific managers were installed on Bering and Copper Islands; the improvement of the Russian Aleut sealers' lot added to the Soviet Union's program for her minority peoples. So, from the ratification of the North Pacific Sealing Convention until 1940, the fur seal of the north knew only increasing security. On October 23rd of that year, a fateful judgment broke the sealing peace.

Indicting the fur seals for damage to her fishing industry, Japan served notice that, a year from that day, she would withdraw from the Convention. Softened by a proposal to negotiate a treaty affording her fisheries more protection, the denunciation made no public stir in the United States. Yet Japan had used her "fisheries" as a political lever too often to have her grievance accepted at its face value, particularly in that world-troubled year. However, the Fish and Wildlife Service optimistically took up the challenge. Scientists arrived at St. Paul Island in the late summer to brand and tag young seals. While they awaited a vessel scheduled to take them south in their wake, on October 23, 1941, the air waves bore a message, broadcast in English, that Japan would, henceforth, wage war against the northern fur seals. For seven weeks the Pribilof Aleuts, ever mindful of the mutilated seal victims of Northeast Point, walked in fear of attack, certain that warfare against the fur seals of the North Pacific would turn into a war against the peoples of the Pacific. Then Japan pounced treacherously on the Pribilof seals' guardians. The rupture of the fur seal Convention had been an alarm few United States citizens had understood.

To afford the seals a degree of safety, Canada and the United States signed an emergency agreement in December 1942. After 1941 the Soviet Union could do little to protect its migrating seals against the hunters Japan dispatched to sea to get urgently needed meat and oil. Brief though this pelagic attack proved— it was prohibited in 1945 by the Occupation Forces—it exacted a fearful toll of seal life. It was Japan, the fur seals' severest critic, who asked the United States on April 7, 1951 to negotiate a new sealing treaty. A few months later the United States invited Canada, Japan, and the Soviet Union to join her in clearing up some unsolved mysteries of North Pacific fur seals' distribution, their migration and feeding habits. Although willing to endorse a new Convention, the Soviet Union declined to participate in the survey, possibly because her herds seemed too depleted to warrant expensive seagoing studies. Biologists from the United States, Canada, and Japan went to sea early in 1952 to pry into the doings of traveling seals.

In Pacific Asiatic waters, the investigators, accompanied by crews of Japan's recently retired veteran sealers, traveled on six oceangoing Japanese harpoon ships, developed since 1941 to increase pelagic sealing efficiency. From a platform extended over the bow of these modern vessels, hunters overlook their swimming targets and, at short range, can shoot seals directly below them, even those swimming under water to escape pursuit. Extremely maneuverable, the tiller-steered harpoon boat zigzags almost as rapidly as a seal tacks in desperate flight. The construction of special mobile, oceangoing, sealing vessels underscores Japan's dependence on the sea for oil and meat; the trained seal fishers are a reminder that the livelihood of a group of Japanese citizens is dislocated by the suspension of pelagic sealing.

Reconnoitering migration lanes along the American coast, researchers of the three nations traveled in two 80-foot purse-seine boats, slow and clumsy vessels in which to pursue traveling seals. No member of the crews had ever hunted the elusive targets of swimming animals.

Shooting seals for study dramatized again the wastefulness of all pelagic hunting. The bodies of 1,823 seals, only 65 per cent of those shot by five crews in Asian waters, were taken aboard. Despite the harpoon ships' mobility, inability to pick up dead bodies before they sank accounted for most of this loss. Of wounded fugitives who got away, some, not mortally injured, may have recovered. A brief specimen-taking foray in 1950 reported a known 6 per cent loss of wounded seals; generally the average is higher. Clumsy boats and amateur sealers hampered the eastern expedition which killed only 817 animals and failed to collect 16 per cent of the slain. No count was attempted of the wounded who escaped.

The contents of almost 3,000 stomachs were analyzed later for clues to fur seal food tastes. They are not finical. Sophisticated travelers, they eat any and all kinds of fish they meet up with on their journeys; along most of the American migration circuit, only unimportant small species. However, briefly, off certain shores at certain times of the year, they consume commercially valuable fish. For instance, along California's shoreline salmon furnished 6 per cent of the homeward-bound migrants' springtime diet, the major part of it farther on, off Oregon. Passing Vancouver Island and Sitka, during May and June, they devoured herring. In stomachs of seals caught in Alaskan waters, however, only traces of unmarketable fish were present. As far as American and Canadian fishermen are concerned, the available evidence indicates that competition with the fur seals is petty, seasonal and, as in all seas, sporadic and accidental, depending on the chance meeting of fish and migrating seal. Future dissections of a larger number of stomachs, and those of seals taken at other seasons of the year, may show, however, that fur seals are more serious competitors of commercial fishermen than they appear now.

As a small island nation, Japan is tragically dependent on her fishing industry to feed her large population. Twice yearly, in spring and in fall, migrating members of all northern clans cross her most productive fishing grounds of Sanriku and Hokkaido. In the early months of the year nearly a third of the transients' diet is food fish. Even though so large a proportion of their diet be small, noncommercial kinds, they are, unfortunately, species that Japan's market fish depend on for survival. While actual breakage of nets and fishing gear by hungry seals seems infrequent, one raddled net may spell tragedy to a poor fisherman; a few torn beyond repair may affect a small fleet's seasonal catch. That so many browse in certain of Japan's ocean pastures for a few months of the year justifies her fears that the sea bears will soon, if they have not already begun, despoil her chief food resource. Japan seems rightfully entitled to the annual recompense the Soviet Union and the United States pay for their seals' dining out.

These 1952 studies and others strengthened the suspicion that only one species of fur seal (*Callorhinus ursinus*) exists in the North Pacific. Comparative anatomical studies, for the first time performed on a large number of specimens, reveal no morphological differentiation between members of the three herds. These findings do not mean that individuals of the Alaskan, Commander and Robben Island populations, although

capable of interbreeding, intermingle and mate freely or frequently. Even if the herds are but three breeding groups of one
species, their members are bound to their birth islands and
their community by a potent homing instinct, feeble in youth
but growing in strength as seals mature, until its discipline inexorably sends them homeward.

But a single example of adult resettlement is known, a bull,
tagged on St. Paul, who set up housekeeping on neighboring
St. George. Certainly if seals changed residence often, more
incidents would be spotted on the Pribilof Islands where seal
identities are most rigorously checked and behavior on the
breeding beaches most scrupulously watched and noted. Innumerable families ruled by Alaskan beachmasters, wearing
their youthful identification mark, have been seen on Pribilof
rookeries year after year; some, tagged or branded or well-
known for conspicuous battle scars, even occupy the same
harem sites season after season. Pribilof-marked bachelors turn
up constantly on the seal drives. Mature members of each clan
evidently keep obediently to the settled itineraries between
their birthplaces and their winter feeding grounds still. Young
fur seals are not so tradition-bound.

In the last 40 years a few branded or tagged Alaskan adolescent strays have turned up on Commander and Robben
Island hauling grounds but never an identifiable breeding-age
deserter on the rookeries, and about 30 per cent of the nonbreeding 3- to 5-year olds, both male and female, in Japanese
waters during spring migration are Pribilof-born. Young Asian
seals may swim with Pribilof companions in American waters
but none have yet been encountered. Russian identification experiments began about 1926 but, to date, not one of their
marked animals has been seen on the Pribilof Islands or in
their vicinity and not one identifiable Russian pelt has turned
up among the 1,500,000 skins taken on the Pribilof Islands between 1930 and 1952. Occasionally, very occasionally, a lone
sea bear loses his way. Three have gone astray in Arctic waters
since 1925; one of them, emaciated by his 2,000 mile swim,

was killed in 1951 in a slightly saline inland lake in the Yukon Territory connected with Mackenzie Bay. Local Eskimos did not recognize the animals; their dialects possess no name for fur seal.

Scientists do not interpret young seal vagabondage as a portent of changing tribal habits. As yet only seals too young to play a role on home-breeding beaches, too young also to have become accustomed to the grooves of ancestral patterns, exercise freedom of choice in selecting winter vacation waters, and range far and wide in search of food or to swim in comfortable currents where the temperatures are neither too cold nor too hot. As soon as maturity awakens the mating instinct, they are conformists. The knowledge that young seals do ramble capriciously and could take up residence on whatever islands they chose, however, conjures up frightening specters of explosive international complications to come. Were older animals to indulge in frequent and seasonal interchange of breeding sites, no nation could claim them as their own. Will the fur seals' nationality eventually become a problem only the United Nations can solve? The outlook is not that depressing. Fur seals are notoriously slow to change their ways. As long as breeding-age animals obey the magnetic pull of instinct and return loyally to their birthplaces to reproduce, any mating between members of the three northern herds which may occur today must be rare and accidental and is not a symptom of pending mass upheaval.

The absence of marked morphological differences between the northern herds is understandable. All pinnipeds have a history of very slow evolutionary change. The climate prevailing on island groups close to the southern limits of the Arctic ice pack affords contemporary sea bears the same cool, humid atmosphere that their common ancestors, on the prowl for breeding grounds, found congenial. No environmental innovation has made bodily modification needful. Development of defense against man on land would necessitate changes of individual or group behavior unless, no other means being found and if circumstances permitted, the further and total reversion to becoming marine mammals, bearing, like whales, their young in the sea instead of on land, were to be hastened.

Poignant is the present disproportion between the censuses of the northern herds. In 1953 the Robben Island population was estimated to be between forty or fifty thousand strong; cautious guesswork credits the Commander Island rookeries with barely double that population. Each spring, according to the very conservative seal count method adopted in 1948, more than a million and a quarter breeding seals return to the Pribilof rookeries; a host augmented, by midsummer, by the birth of over half a million pups. As the summer draws toward its close, there is an influx of some yearlings and other adolescent visitors, so, despite the killing of about 65,000 young males for their skins, the Pribilof seal total nears the two million mark. Several biologists theorize that, chiefly because the food supply in waters within commuting distance of the mother seals is limited, the Pribilof dynasty may have reached its maximum. Other arguments—no fur seal theory ever dies—have been dusted off after decades of retirement to bolster the opinion that the Pribilof herd has reached its maximum growth under existing conditions: that the present fecundity of rookeries is so great that the seals cannot find space on the congested rocks to mate and reproduce so the birth rate is about to decline, and that population growth is being checked because more pups are trampled to death in overcrowded harems. Why the seals cannot spread out to beaches their forefathers occupied a few generations ago has not been explained by advocates of these hypotheses, who may dismiss accounts of former plenitude as myth. Should the phantom of overpopulation become real, and hungry seals lay waste the fishing resources of any country, judicious increase of commercial killing can reduce their depredation. But the proof of spoliation must be incontrovertible; the increase truly judicious.

Having weathered all criticism, that last target of Henry Elliott's ire, the Fouke Fur Company, is still the Department of

Interior's agent to process and auction American sealskins; its
only rival one small London furrier. To compete in the fashion
mart, a rivalry Elliott did not foresee as spur to prevent monopolistic paralysis, the Company experiments with new dyes
and keeps the Alaskan sealskin coat in style. The major portion
of the world's sealskin harvest is sent to its St. Louis plant, in
addition to the Pribilof catch, a few hundred skins from Canada
taken lawfully by Indian hunters, Lobos Islands pelts from Uruguay (5,400 skins in 1957), and skins from the Union of South
Africa (29,300 of them in 1957). How the Soviet Union han-
dles its small Commander catch of about 5,000 skins has not
been publicized.

On February 9, 1957 the United States, Canada, Japan, and
the Soviet Union signed the regnant Interim Convention for the
Conservation of North Pacific Fur Seals, embodying all the
main guarantees and prohibitions of its 1911 forerunner.

A spirit of co-operation and genuine interest in the seals'
safety animates the agreement, demonstrated by decisions to
co-ordinate all investigations of fur seal mysteries, even exchange scientific personnel, and to create a North Pacific Seal
Commission, composed of a representative of each signatory,
to cope with problems the fur seal may yet present. The Commission will study the findings of pooled and joint research and
adopt, if the decision be unanimous, different sealing practices
new information may indicate are needful, even sit in judgment
on the animals if they are brought to trial for trespassing, property damage, or other misdemeanors.

The Soviet Union may suspend seal killing on the Commander and the Robben Islands—the latter under her management since the war with Japan ended, providing either herd's
census fall below 50,000 seals. Should a *zapusk* be necessary
for either Soviet herd, the Commission may halt western Pacific
pelagic research.

Of signal consequence to the seals themselves are the generous terms of the ransom to be paid countries whose citizens
once made a living from pelagic sealing. Those which own no

seal islands, Canada—and since the war—Japan, are each to receive, yearly, fifteen per cent of the sealskins taken by the United States and the Soviet Union. Painful lessons have convinced the United States that the sea bear must be attended and subjected to close inspection during the two thirds of its life it spends away from land, and its conduct, appetite, and ranging habits scrutinized and pried into until, stripped bare of all privacy, its every reflex, whim, or possible divergence from group mores is understood and become predictable, and no seemingly inexplicable and obscure actions can spell out new riddles to create human misunderstandings. To solve fur seal enigmas for all time—it is hoped—present pelagic studies, limited by the Convention to expeditions in a Government vessel, supervised by that Government's representatives, and specimen-killing restricted by specific stipulations, should suffer no interruption. To guarantee their unbroken progress the United States has underwritten, according to a schedule prepared to meet various foreseeable contingencies, Soviet indemnities to Japan and Canada should the Russian catch decline below the present norm or her sealing be suspended—eventualities to which Asiatic specimen-taking would, undoubtedly, have contributed. In case of *zapuski* on all Soviet seal islands, the United States will, for example, give Japan and Canada another 375 sealskins apiece each year of the suspension. Despite generous indemnity and the United States' promise to make good any payments the Soviet Union is unable to make, it seems as if her recent pelagic sealing has been too important to Japan's economy for that country to relinquish its benefits happily.

Because it was the Japanese Government which insisted on the provision that any signer may call for special review of a regulation and, if dissatisfied with the outcome of such a hearing, may serve notice to terminate the Convention nine months later. Japan's reluctance to be bound to a promise of permanent security for the fur seal on the high seas rests on a genuine fear lest its depredation of her food fishes increase. Nevertheless, the seals' maritime insurance policy is not danger-proof as long as this loophole exists. Only the co-operative efforts of the United States and the Soviet Union to keep track of damage their grazing seals may do to Japan's fish resources and their willingness to concede her equitable indemnity for boarding them during migration can prevent this flaw widening to be a breach of seal peace. That the sea bear never be unscrupulously used again as a pretext to sunder national friendships will also be as strongly guaranteed as humanly possible by such Russian-American co-operation.

Approximately $325,000 worth of Pribilof skins, worth about $50 apiece today, will be divided equally between Canada and Japan each year. This contribution and its Commissioner's salary, in addition to the regular expenditures for patrolling, management, and research, is but little for the United States to pay to safeguard the Pribilof fur seal while preserving amity with other Pacific nations. Especially since, properly handled, the fur seal foots the bill.

21

The Sealskin Curtain Rises

After 1867 the valuable pelt of the Alaskan fur seal was a thick screen behind which generations of Aleut sealers lived, worked, and died in obscurity: their civil status and rights as American citizens ignored, their economic compensation meager and farcical, their educational and health services inferior and deficient—their very existence unknown to most of their fellow Americans.

That this small pocket of un-American feudalism endured so long on the Seal Islands was due, principally, to the small size of the Aleut communities (The total population of St. Paul and St. George Islands is less than five hundred individuals.), and their dependence for a livelihood on the fur seals while resident on isolated islands out-of-bounds as wildlife reservations to all but authorized management personnel, experts on animal matters disinterested in or ill-trained to grapple with the complexities of governing human beings. Aleuts had no voice in their own affairs, no hope for change because, their historical rights ignored and forgotten, they were being manipulated by the formula that they were Government wards—not citizens. Custom sanctioned local paternalistic supervision. Pressed by sealing exigencies, harassed supervisors paid little heed to uncomplaining workmen. Under Company or Government management, the feudal pattern never altered. The sealers existed, worked and died—in the fur seals' shadow. An occasional enlightened functionary strove to change the social order, especially after 1910, but either efforts were futile, or reforms inadequate or fleeting. Few Fish and Wildlife officers took note of changing Aleut customs, attitudes and ambitions during the years preceding Pearl Harbor. Caught off guard when informed that the Pribilofs must be evacuated, and fearful lest the sealers' attachment to their birthplaces and sense of group unity would prove frailer than the fur seals', the useful position the Aleuts occupied in the general scheme of Pribilof life and seal management became appallingly clear. If there were no native-born inhabitants bound by ties of affection to their Pribilof homes, who would service the modern villages, keep the motors running, the electric light plant functioning, the plumbing in order? How could imported workmen be compensated to endure the loneliness of island life? Service officials' fears that their ill-paid submissive laborers would be weaned away from their homes and jobs by higher salaries, pleasanter working conditions, and other enticements of the outside world, were baseless, it transpired, but their basic apprehension was realized. The old order was gone. The fur seals survived the war with no drastic change of their life pattern; that of the sealers, shattered by events, was transformed according to a more democratic design.

If date or decisive deed be needed to demarcate the break with the past, it was the day, two weeks after the Japanese bombed Dutch Harbor in June 1942, when the Pribilof Islands' entire population was rescued from the war zone to be dumped in abandoned fishing and mining camps on Admiralty Island, not far from Juneau as a sea gull flies, but safely removed from regular neighborly contact with Alaskan towns and villages. Crowded into the dilapidated, ill-furnished camps of Funter Bay, Aleuts found even survival difficult. Many died, not, as apologists claimed, from the "climate," but as the results of overcrowding, poor diet, and generally bad living conditions, which favored the spread of infections. As many sealers as could left the camps to work, for the first time for regular wages and for private employers, on boats or in Alaskan towns. An Army order

first blasted away a bastion of their feudalism. As citizens—
citizens!—the young men were to come to the aid of their country and register for military service. Back in Washington bewildered Fish and Wildlife chiefs summoned their lawyers only to
find it had been written long ago in 1867 that the native Alaskans, the true owners of the territory the Czar was selling to
the United States, had, according to the deed of sale, been
granted American citizenship, a status reaffirmed by later legislation. Only when all citizens were called to arms, the litter
of ancient falsehood and current misunderstandings was swept
away and the stigmatizing label, "Government ward," exposed
as legally invalid. Aleut despair, which that degrading label had
fostered for decades, evaporated; hope for restoration of their
human dignity was kindled. One by one other barriers against
their exercise of civil rights crumbled. As if coming of age,
these Americans voted. Young men went off to war; younger
children attended Indian Office schools. For the first time sealers' children brought home high school diplomas, even entered
college.

Experiences in Southeastern Alaska robbed the sealers of
one cherished illusion. They discovered that discrimination
against native American minorities was not a Pribilof phenomenon. To some new acquaintances, they were still "just natives,"
but the condescending phrase had lost most of its venom once
their citizenship had been rediscovered and acknowledged.
Natives, truly, but native-born American citizens, so they could
at least protect themselves when discrimination exceeded legal
bounds. Insight they gained, through meeting American descendants of other native peoples, into the whole troubled clash
of their country's racial problems. Strange and bewildering the
recollections they carried back to their islands—a medley of
facts, disillusion, and hope—and a determined ambition to
found a new way of life.

Because, when the islands were again safe for habitation,
most sealers and their families migrated expectantly homeward.
The long hard job of reconstruction began. Bureaucratic inertia

and fear of social change capitulated slowly and reluctantly before the pressing realities of new conditions and the Islanders' insistence on being treated as ordinary citizens and Service workmen. Only contentment with living and working conditions could, henceforth, keep sealer citizens at home and at work. Threats to revoke his residence right and deny him re-entry are no longer used to detain an Aleut on his birthplace. Prewar isolation, when only five ships a year called at the islands, was shattered by the introduction of airplane service; postal communication with the world is swift and regular. The ban that no student could attend local primary schools after his sixteenth birthday, in force until 1942, was withdrawn. Young people go "Outside" to school; Island grade schools have been improved.

Seal hunting is the one thread of continuity linking Aleut generations from the epoch of their hardy primitive independence through two centuries of serving foreign masters to the present. Long before 1942, however, sealing had become but one task in a year-round schedule of eight-hour-day labors. Only during the foggy morning hours of each brief killing season, the men took up their long staffs, symbols of their inherited office. As carpenters, mechanics, plumbers, workmen performing all the jobs maintenance of a modern town demands, no budget increase had been requested to requite this skilled regular work. Pribilof villages were continually modernized, their facilities for efficiency and comfort improved but no idea of paying the Aleut building and maintenance crews proper wages entered official minds. Without even such lip service as Russian colonial paymasters rendered the ideal of fair compensation, the unwieldy, outmoded system of the 1880's, modified without altering its structure, had creaked on. Bureaucratic blindness and the notion that mere "wards" were not entitled to the same pay for work performed as true American citizens, preserved the confusing system of compensation in goods, services, and, the only outright payment of cash, the annual bonus—its very name was a giveaway—for seal killing.

The nature and worth of the Aleuts' labor not being taken into account, food, fuel, and clothing rations had been doled out to them (Often much less than allotment lists prescribed, but what ward dare question amount or quality of his guardians' handout?), and insufficient housing furnished. Medical care and schooling of variable quality had been administered as if benevolent charity. In 1950 this muddled system was partially scrapped, but because the question of compensation was not tackled afresh from the norm of just pay for labor performed— as if hiring new workers, and in accordance with Alaskan pay standards, the wage reform plan finally ironed out is oddly complex and imperfect.

Aside from the inadequacy of the salaries, the present wage schedule's greatest defects seem the retention of the outmoded complicated classification of workmen, according to the old sealing gang divisions, into thirteen classes, and the fact that what is now officially called an "incentive bonus" for taking sealskins, is still figured at the rate of 40 cents a skin, the rate paid 80 years ago. As Government workers, the sealers are now pressing for the abolition of this system, which relegates them to the status of unclassified civil service employees, and classification in proper civil service categories with the establishment of the sealing bonus—at a rate more commensurate with the value of the sealskin today—as true recompense for their sealing labors. They ask quite naturally why, if they are governed by Civil Service Commission rules, they are not entitled to correct civil service status—and pay. The decision to kill no Pribilof foxes in recent winters has caused a further reduction in income, especially because the bonus paid for each skin is $3.50, far higher than the sealskin bonus rate.

In addition to the annual wage, which fluctuates from $3,016 for a very few men classified as skilled worker A-3 to $988 for the unskilled worker classified as D-1, the sealers are given rent-free houses and 150 kilowatt hours of electricity as part of their remuneration. Most families use and pay for more electricity, and all householders are responsible for the upkeep and repair of their homes and for heating them. Resident Service employees from the States pay $180 a year for utilities, including heating their much larger houses while the sealers, forced to buy all their coal or oil from the Service, spend as much as $400 a year only for fuel to heat their much smaller cottages. Afforded an opportunity to choose between coal and oil heating, many families elected to buy and install oil heaters only to find themselves unable to buy oil. Because there was a large supply of coal on the islands and some officials deemed the oil heaters unsafe, the Service arbitrarily decided to withhold oil shipments until the coal on hand was consumed. A promise of adequate oil stocks for the winter of 1959-60 was finally obtained by the intercession of one of Alaska's new Senators, E. L. Bartlett.

The most profound and far-reaching change was the introduction of local self-government under elected Village Councils when the communities of St. George and St. Paul received their Charters and By-Laws as villages incorporated under the Indian Reorganization Act. They won, too, the right to have their own lawyers and be affiliated with national organizations, such as the Alaska Native Brotherhood, dedicated to solving American Indian problems by legislative means.

Revolutionary as these reversals of old ways may be, no Pribilof Utopia has been created. Learning to be self-governing proceeds slowly, a zigzagging course of trial and error with blunders too often predominant as sealers and officials learn to work together on a new footing, as management and labor rather than master and serf or, at its former best, as guardian and ward. The main stumbling block to harmonious solution of all local problems is the reluctance, almost the refusal, of the Fish and Wildlife Service to deal with the sealers as an organized body.

Throughout the correspondence over the issues of adequate fuel supplies and wage adjustments, Service officers constantly plead that individual sealers with whom these matters were discussed personally were amenable to official opinion. They seem to avoid negotiating with the Village Council or the community

St. Louis Workmen in Pribilof Blubbering Plant

Aleuts Salting Down Seal Furs, St. Paul Island

workers as a group. Ignoring the existence of these Councils will not resolve acute local problems or make for Pribilof peace but will only intensify present antagonisms or create new ones.

Changes would have engendered less animosity and created fewer new problems had the then incumbent, responsible, top-level Fish and Wildlife Service heads called on social anthropologists to be advisers and intermediaries as soon as the Pribilofs were reoccupied. Failure to be as scientific and objective about social problems as about biological ones has left tensions that could have been resolved easily soon after the sealers returned home. Social anthropologists could still contribute to Pribilof growth because both groups have much to learn: the Aleuts that they must be patient but not too long enduring and must not succumb to hopelessness or let their manliness be drained away by breathing in the miasma of former socially degrading attitudes. The officials must shed their patronizing paternalistic attitudes and habits of command and learn to negotiate with the sealers' spokesmen in a normal American democratic way. Some local managers mourn the good old days when sealers were as docile as seals and agents undisputed dictators, wielding arbitrary power in matters now passed to the control of Village Councils. Formerly an agent was judge and jury who punished petty misdoings and infractions of regulations which the Councils settle today. Any appeal against his decisions to his Washington superiors had to be given to him to transmit! Elected village policemen are inclined to wink at their workmates' and neighbors' pecadillos, an understandable leniency which irritates less sympathetic Service personnel.

On the other hand, critics complain of symptoms of healthy initiative, that, for instance, too many sealers are becoming business-minded and have opened stores locally, coffee shops, even ice cream parlors. One entrepreneur, thanks to more regular plane service, offers frequent movie shows. Free enterprise is emerging from feudal serfdom. Not wholly free however. There are permanent drawbacks to residing on Island wildlife closes. The villagers' Charters prohibit business or other activities which might interfere in any way with the lives, protection, and utilization of the natural denizens of these animal reservations. No Privilovian can, for instance, erect a hotel and entice tourists to view the exciting panorama of seal beaches.

Remnants of the first long-vanished alien culture the Aleuts absorbed still color village life with traditional Russian ceremonies and foods at Easter, Christmas, and on other religious festivals as well as at weddings and funerals. Christian and family names are Russian. "Name days" are celebrated as well as American birthdays. The Russian Orthodox Church, its presence protected on the Pribilofs by the Treaty of the Transfer of Alaska to the United States, imparted to generations of sealers spiritual strength to endure the long period of exploitation and isolation from 1867 to 1942. Consequently Aleuts have more than a religious attachment to this church, and but few individuals have been tempted to join other denominations. Nothing except the Aleut language, which fewer and fewer young people speak fluently, remains of their ancestral culture —and even that is corrupted and marred by the addition of foreign words, first Russian and now, and increasingly, English ones. In all other respects, the sealers and their families are, as they have been for decades, Americans in taste and outlook. Unlike the inhabitants of many isolated Alaskan mainland villages, the transition from being Territorial citizens to being citizens of the forty-ninth state calls for no special education in Americanism.

Aleut efforts to perfect and maintain Pribilof democracy continue parallel to other Alaskans' transformation of the former territory into the forty-ninth state. As the State of Alaska becomes firmly integrated with national life, the story of the fur seals and their centuries-old guardians, the Aleuts, will become widely known as an interesting chapter of American history. On the national scene, the Aleuts are emerging from behind the sealskin curtain, not as primitives capable only of clubbing harmless fur seals but as well-knit communities of hard-working citizens with a tragic and romantic heritage due to the geographical accident of being the fur seals' neighbors. Still as proud of their traditional calling of sealers as of their skills as workmen or professionals, these native American inhabitants of beautiful and valuable Alaskan Islands are determined to maintain their identity in the villages of their forefathers without relinquishing their right to be a part of the mainstream of their country's history.

22

Roundup of Seals
and Sealing News

If peace endure and treaties be honored, no danger threatens the northern fur seals at sea today and, if current sealing practices endure, no serious one confronts them on their natal islands. The most marketable skins are still the silky pelts of three- and four-year-old bachelors, males too young to breed. Because of the seals' polygamous nature, a large percentage of them are, fortunately for the species' survival, expendable. The adolescent males' habit of congregating in large pods, gentlemen's clubs as it were, and their docility and harmlessness make them easy to capture. Killing them is a swift, probably painless, operation. As long as sufficient males are permitted to grow up to become breeding bulls, the Pribilof tribe will flourish on its breeding islands.

Methodical and efficient as the Pribilof roundups and killings are, the furred rodeo and the subsequent ritual of the killing field unfold in bizarre drama under the foggy Bering Sea sky. Because their hauling grounds lie between the inviolable rookery boundaries, surrounding the bachelors occasions some alarm among adjacent harems. On St. Paul Island, where most Alaskan fur seals breed, the daily assault, from late June to late July, rotates from one seal beach to another in a schedule which gives the breeders five days of tranquillity—seal beach tranquillity that is. During the respite, other bachelors, unaware they are jeopardizing their lives, move into the vacated territory.

In the coolest hours of the day, usually at three o'clock in the morning—one or two areas are sealed at dusk—Aleut sealers, Fish and Wildlife Service overseers, and Fouke Fur Company agents assemble for the roundup; the sealers armed with long wooden poles. No matter the nature of his year-round village job, every able-bodied Aleut is there. Only an islander born can hunt and kill the fur seals, an inherited responsibility in which the Aleuts take great pride. As chief actors they perform many roles in the shifting scenes of the sealing drama. As the play opens, under cover of darkness and fog they scurry cautiously, keeping upwind of the seals, over the rough terrain along the water front. At each hauling ground, a group breaks off, and shouting, beating the rocks with their poles, the sealers charge inland toward the unsuspecting bachelors. Escape seaward barred by noisy attackers, flight to right or left disputed by hostile bulls, the bachelors stampede toward the rear— straight inland. Enraged bulls roar warnings and lunge savagely at any who seek a short cut to safety across their harems. Behind the fleeing animals the sealers advance implacably. Soon all along the beach the scene repeats itself as scouting sealers surprise and rout other pods. The air vibrates with the harsh gasping of the fleeing, roars of embattled bulls, sealers' shouts, and the ominous thudding of their poles on stone. Tumult in the rookeries increases. Excited cows, indifferent to their bleating young, dodge about their harems seeking egress. Bulls rear up bellowing to repel trespassers and subdue panic-stricken cows. Seizing their wives with their teeth, the bulls sling them, often bleeding from deep gashes, back on their home rocks. Infuriated by the pandemonium, neighboring beachmasters turn on each other to do battle. Once the hunters have passed, they are forgotten. Agitation on the breeding beach soon ebbs to its normal frenzy.

When the captive pods arrive outside seal beach territory, their pursuers head them toward the nearest grassy flats. At

Reef Rookery on St. Paul the journey is indeed the last mile and a little longer; the other killing grounds are closer to the beaches they service.

No sooner does a seal pod reach open space than its members rush headlong together, flopping like a pile of slithering, freshly caught fish. As some animals struggle to the top, those below push upward and surmount them. Their former attackers, transformed into watchful solicitous herdsmen, prepare to drive their flock to the killing field. Patiently they guard the furry maelstrom while sleek bodies spurt upward as from a fountain, fall back to be submerged among their fellows. One who gets clear of the melee is steered back by a gentle tap of a sealer's pole. When panic lessens or fatigue overwhelms them, the bachelors stop their insane jostling and subside. Meekly then, in response to gentle prodding and their driver's rock-tapped signals, they flipflop over the rough ground. Nudging and pushing, they scramble along, trying to outdistance the harsh sounds. A few spirited ones may snap at hovering poles, feeble displays of annoyance which are not true resistance to their captors. Beating an intermittent tattoo on the rocks, whistling or clapping their hands, the drivers keep the seals moving toward their destination. Sometimes—a macabre touch lost on the fur seals, the drivers use seal scapulae as cymbals. The Aleuts manipulate their long clubs gracefully to keep laggards on the move and push runaways back into line.

A fur seal has sweat glands only in its flippers and cannot long endure strenuous activity on land. Skilled drivers let the seals choose their own pace. Frequent rests are permitted. When a lead seal drops down panting, his tongue out like a weary dog, the drivers pause too. Oncoming seals pile up again in disorder until they realize they may rest. Almost before the stragglers drop to their bellies, the vanguard is moving on of its own accord. Soon the whole furry mass is forging ahead again with its abrupt choppy rhythm, pod following pod in disorderly file.

Conspicuously overtired animals will be cut out of line.

Usually, so strong is their peculiar gregariousness, that the re-
prieved fight to continue the Death March. They resist exclu-
sion from the crowd more stubbornly than attack. If rejects
have the strength to reach the sea, their chance of survival is
good. Some die, however, before reaching the water. Constant
vigilance is exercised to prevent exhaustion and overheating
because pelts of animals dying from overheating—called road
skins—spoil within a couple of hours; the pelt becomes slimy,
the guard hairs loose. After the day's catch has been skinned,
search parties comb the area between the sea and the Death
Parade route to collect all dying or dead seals before the furs
become useless. A high roadskin count is a disgrace that proud
sealers avoid.

The cast assembled on the killing ground, named in the Aleut
tongue *Un'gisxalgaq,* the Place without Hope, the drama of
fur-taking begins. Protective herders turn killers. Others pick
up their tools to tackle the specialized jobs of seal skinning.
An onlooker's first impression, due to noise and movement, is
of a chaotic brawl. Gradually the pattern of machinelike labor
and efficient work division becomes apparent. The mechanical
rhythm of the 20th-century assembly line dominates this factory
in the field.

A pod, driven on the grassy expanse of that open-air factory,
is immediately ringed round by sealers. Their cudgels, no longer
batons, are become death-dealing weapons. A single blow on its
extraordinarily thin skull almost always kills a seal. While clubs
rise and fall with fatal precision on seal heads, one man twirls
a bright tin lard pail on the tip of a six-foot pole. Its clatter
and glitter drive the seals once more to huddle desperately
together as if contact of body against body were defense against
danger. This workman is a fantastic clown as he leaps about,
brandishing his strange toy in midair. Deftly he spears the can
into the wriggling heap, separating the seals so that clubbers
can strike them one by one. With a swift thrust, his can shoves
an unwanted seal away. The clatter of the revolving bucket
clangs above the bachelors' snorting, whistling, and puffing, and

the sharp crackling thuds of fracturing skulls. Inexorably the pail wards off each rejected seal bent on return to useless suicide. Spurned males, too young or too old, or females accidentally picked up in the raid seem insanely obsessed to throw themselves under the killers' clubs. Other animal species would strive to flee such a welter of bodies and noise, but these victims of exaggerated gregariousness struggle to remain with their perishing companions. Outwitted at last, redeemed seals usually sit down in the grass a few yards from the bloody, steaming carcasses of their kin to fan themselves nonchalantly with their flippers, their obsession to stay with the crowd suddenly snuffed out. They sit, indifferent, blind, and deaf to the nearby slaughter, until, refreshed, they wander off toward the sea.

As a seal collapses from the blow to his skull, men snatch his limp body to lay out as one of an ordered row of ten corpses. Instantly, with a single lethal jab of his knife, one of the killing gang completes the execution. If the club has only stunned him, the seal remains unconscious, except in rare instances, until this *coup de grâce* is administered. While the killing proceeds, a man passes along each row measuring the warm, palpitating bodies. His notebook-armed partner jots down the dimensions shouted to him. Legally a skin must now be between 41 and 45 inches long. Dried ones suffer too many alterations to be trustworthy evidence of their deceased owners' age. Only these on-the-spot measurements establish accurately the true size, and so the age, of the animals killed—as Elliott only too scathingly demonstrated in the halls of Congress decades ago.

In the stabbers' wake, cutters slit the pelts around the head and the flippers and straight down the abdomen to loosen them. Like their shadows, follow men armed with large, two-pronged forks. Each pins down a carcass at the neck and stands on its head to hold the body stationary. Immediately workmen attach a forcepslike tool, a nipper, to the pelt's edge at the neck. These nippers eliminate damage due to human carelessness or fatigue. A slashed pelt has no market value and even the most expert knife wielder has accidents after spending cramped hours skinning hundreds of seals before their skins spoil. Grasping the nippers firmly, the skinners take a few steps backward and the carcass is stripped bare, the skin in perfect condition. The swish of ripping silk whips the air as skins come off. Swooping down on the denuded bodies other workers snip off the leathery flippers with a single deft snap of especially designed clippers resembling overgrown pruning shears. Left on bodies sent to the By-Products Plant, flippers cook up into a glue which clogs machinery and ruins the seal meal and oil. Japan used to convert them into gelatin.

Boy sealer apprentices quickly drag the raw, deflippered carcasses from underfoot. Stacked untidily along both sides of the skinning space, they become the border of a lane wide enough for waiting trucks to enter. Meanwhile other boys pounce on the skins to spread them on clean grass to cool. As a truck is driven slowly up the carcass-lined path, two men on each side spear the bodies with long-handled salmon pughs and toss them aboard.

Once the first row of ten bodies is stretched out, work progresses without interruption. No one pauses or falters. Each man performs his task with swift machinelike accuracy. Clubs rise and fall monotonously. The tin pail flashes and shrieks. Row after row, bodies are dealt out on the grass as smoothly as cards on a table surface. Knives descend and red jets spurt from quivering bodies. Cutters kneel and cut the outlines of the pelts. They rise, wheel toward the next bodies, and kneel again. Other men spring forward with the big forks to pin down and immobilize the bodies. Skinners bend to attach the nippers, straighten up and walk backward in unison. The grotesque scissors of the clipper men snip off the flippers as impatient hands reach to drag the carcasses off the killing center. Hovering boys snatch up the skins and lay them on the grass. The trucks crawl along the gory roadway, each filled in a few seconds with its gruesome load. Less than four hours after the hunt begins, thousands of sealskins are ready to be made into furs.

Seal apathy and seal folly rob the killing field of horror. No

seal fights back. No seal recoils from the smell of his com-
rades' fresh-spilt blood or mourns a playmate's death. It is not
a true instinct of self-defense which sends the seals rushing
madly together in time of danger and confusion. Their safety
lies not in numbers. Senseless bunching together makes them
easy prey. Did they scatter, each animal bent solely on saving
himself, the hunt would be more hazardous. Hunters would
need long-range weapons and, because a bullet-scarred pelt
would be useless, skill as marksmen to single out and hit one
bobbing head among a fleeing mob. The fur seals' perverse
gregariousness, then, fosters a delusion which costs them their
lives. But while that impulse to rush together betrays individuals, it does operate—as long as man takes wise advantage of
it—to preserve the species. It would be ridiculous to claim fur
seals deliberately make scapegoats of superfluous bachelors but,
from man's point of view, they are the victims sacrificed to pay
for the safety of their tribe. So the land hunter can be—and is
at present—a kind of cattle drover rounding up his fin-footed
herd which has cost neither money nor time to feed and shelter
and from which he can easily select only those animals most
market-worthy and profitable. Although their preposterous so-
ciality was not evolved to save them from human foes, fur seals
are not so retarded that they lack aptitude to learn to protect
their lives. At sea self-preservative traits are conspicuous. They
have developed agile tactics of escape from marine enemies—
stratagems which stand them in poor stead only against pelagic
sealers' firearms. An individual seal is either a lone sea voyager
or a member of a small scattered band. To guard his own life,
he dives deep—as deep as 250 feet below the surface. He swims
under water. He darts and swerves in dizzy designs to outwit
pursuit. Since the seal has been intelligent enough to devise
ways to escape his fiercest natural foe, the killer whale, at sea,
why has he not modified his behavior to guard against his more
predatory land enemy?

Long ago the seals' ancestors chose, for climatic comfort,
to breed only on inclement islands where man is still a new-

comer. Their frenzied rushing together is probably only an involuntary reaction of fear to danger too novel still after little more than two centuries of being hunted on land, a period too brief for the species to understand its vulnerability or the threat to its existence and adopt new self-defensive tactics. The fur seals' seemingly gregarious behavior when attacked on land, is, then, response to primal ignorance, a hysterical spasm of recoil from the unknown.

Since their sheeplike obstinacy to follow one another, even to death beneath the lethal clubs, seems a monstrous kind of masochism, the sea bears' execution excites no compassion. The dexterous precision and swift skilled movements of the sealers weave a ballet of action which leaves a deeper impression on the onlooker than the death of such insentient animals.

Flensing and curing sealskins is an island industry managed by the Fouke Fur Company. Inside their buildings, as on the killing field, the work routine has its rhythm which begins when the first trucks roll up to washhouse windows. Skins are pitched directly through them into huge tanks of sea brine piped in from the Bering Sea. Workmen, sheathed in rubber boots, swish them about, then fork them up onto a platform to be rinsed before immersing them in other tanks of clean sea water. After soaking 10 days in this brine, the 10-pound fresh skin weighs only 4 or 5 pounds. The dark ill-lit shed, the shadowy figures, the hissing torrents of water, the revolting stew of churning skins, the penetrating chill dampness, and the stench of bloody raw pelts create a Hadean gloom.

In contrast with the washsheds, the blubbering rooms exude light and seem comfortable, although their temperature is not much warmer. The dull scrubbing sound of blubber knives scraping off the seal fat blurs all other noise.

Blubbering is generally done by experienced workmen brought to the islands from St. Louis by the Company. They bob up and down ludicrously as they shave skins draped blubber-side-up over sturdy, rounded wooden beams. These flensing forms resemble toy ironing boards set up washboardwise, waist-high from the floor. The workmen shove their two-handled knives downward in quick, precise movements designed to avoid slicing the pelt. The blubber they remove is made into a special oil the Fouke Fur Company uses later for softening salted sealskins. The flensers scrape off the fat, trim the rough edges of the flipper holes, toss the cleaned skin over their shoulders to the top of a table behind them, and, usually without turning their heads, grab a fatty one from the table's lower shelf, and start work on it. They pause only to clean greasy knives. Wiping one on his canvas apron, a blubberer seems about to commit hari-kari. Blubbering is limited to three or four hours a day, the most a strong man can endure of such backbreaking, arm-numbing toil before becoming too fatigued to control his knife.

Little boys run busily about the room removing blubbered skins, replenishing stocks of unflensed ones. Cable trucks carry wet skins from the washhouse to the blubbering room; flensed ones from the latter place to be pressed in a handworked mangle. Another conveyor bears the neatly folded, wrung-out pelts across the yard to the salthouse. Once more the skins go into vats, each layer thickly covered with rough salt crystals. In ten days they are dry enough to pack for shipment to St. Louis to be transformed, after many more laborious processes, into elegant furs, romantically named Safari, Matara, and Kitovi.

Packers work in teams of three. Clustered about a barrel, the actual packer stands between two men who powder the inner surfaces of the dried skins with a handful of boric acid and fold them into compact rolls. After depositing a few layers of skins, sprinkling salt over each layer, the packer hops into the barrel, and, as if treading grapes for wine, tamps them tightly into place.

Conversion of carcasses into oil and meat in the By-Products Plant is a minor fur seal industry run by the Fish and Wildlife Service. The shredded coarse brown substance which emerges from the cookers is shoveled into a pressing machine. Some

40,000 gallons of the molasseslike oil expressed from this meal are sold annually in the States, mainly to cosmetic manufacturers. A small quantity of the 350 tons of meal produced each summer is winter food for the famous Pribilof foxes. The rest is sent to hatcheries and other wildlife reservations to be both fish and animal food, or sold at public auction in Seattle.

While Pribilof sealing keeps its present ordered way, the herd will continue to procreate normally and maintain or even increase its population. Annual income will remain commensurate with the $20,000,000 net profit the United States earned from its allotment of the 2,000,000 sealskins taken during the first 45 years of Government-managed sealing. The yearly payments of skins to Canada and Japan will be large enough to buy the fur seals' safe passage at sea.

Aside from man, perils which beset the fur seals on land are few and fairly innocuous. No epidemic of pneumonia, bronchial pneumonia and peritonitis, a few cases of which have been detected, or other infectious disease has, within historical times, occurred on the rookeries. The most deadly menace, attacking only pups, is the hookworm, its ravages occasionally reaching calamitous proportions. Recently, as in 1954, it has killed as many as a fifth of the season's newborn. Anemia due to hookworm infestation also weakens the pups' resistance to microbes and virus infection. Fish and Wildlife scientists are testing methods of disinfecting the pups' sandy playgrounds which harbor hookworm larvae and eggs. It is expected that this plague will be controlled, if not eradicated, soon.

Pups die from congenital deficiencies. Abandoned, motherless ones die of starvation, a less frequent casualty since nursing mothers, protected at sea, suffer only the vicissitudes of natural accidents. Greedy nurslings who gorge themselves when their mothers have been detained too long at sea may die of overeating; a few are trampled to death by the bulls. About half of each season's pups survive the hazards they run on land and sea during their first year; some thirty per cent reach their third birthday. But insignificant are all known natural causes of death compared to the potential menace of man the hunter.

Having redeemed her record of former neglect and exploitation of Alaskan fur seals and undertaken to democratize the lives of Alaskan sealers, the United States is now the chief trustee of all fur seals in international negotiations and the scrupulous summer host and caretaker of the Pribilof herd. After nearly a hundred years of proprietorship, the United States has set its Pribilof house in order and merits its present honorable role as global fur seal champion.

But the United States is only as reliable as its citizens. It was the zeal of ardent, even sentimental, conservationists, such as Hornaday and Elliott, which fired Americans to make sure that fur seal welfare should be of primary concern, profit-taking secondary. American public opinion alone will prevent Government agencies slipping back into lethargic routines, preserve the strange and fascinating sea bear from extinction, and prevent its silver fleece from becoming ever again a source of bitter contention between men and between nations.

Index